Collegiate Solutions

A College Planning Roadmap

ISBN: 978-0-6152-2427-5

Troy A. Hatcher, CCPS

Biography & Fact Sheet

Author, speaker and entrepreneur, Troy A. Hatcher, CCPS may be contacted by:

Email: Hatcher@CSILLC.org
Website: www.CSILLC.org
Phone: (800) 306-6340
Mail: 120 W. Main St., Suite 405, Van Wert, OH 45891

Dedicated to helping families build and execute sound financial plans that satisfy college goals without sacrificing the dream of a secure retirement.

Offering advanced college planning strategies to my clients which include cash flow and financial modeling, while maximizing eligibility for merit and need-based financial aid. Additional expertise in grants and scholarships. I have working knowledge of financial instruments for education and how they affect aid. I also counsel students with career planning and college selection. This in turn helps parents and grandparents with college bound students reduce their cost of college and achieve their goals in attending the University of their Choice.

I am proud to be one of the select few advisors to receive the designation of Certified College Planning Specialist (CCPS). I hold a Bachelor of Science degree in Aerotechnology from Bowling Green State University, as well as various insurance licenses.

Areas of Expertise:
- College Funding Strategies

- Wealth Accumulation

- Retirement Funding

- Asset Allocation

- Cash Flow Analysis

- Insurance Strategies

TABLE OF CONTENTS

Introduction
A Roadmap to College and Retirement Funding

Saving for college and retirement is a daunting task for most families. Some families try to save for both at the same time, but most families are unable to accomplish this without sacrificing their current lifestyle or going broke. For the families that must decide which one to save for, the answer is simple. Retirement funding should take priority. Retirement is the dog, college is the tail.

Since college is a more immediate problem and involves their children, many parents fund college at the expense of their retirement. This can lead to disastrous retirement consequences. Therefore, unless you are secure in your retirement plan, you should not consider saving for your children's college costs. Children can borrow for the entire cost of college and thus, not jeopardize your retirement. You may not be able to borrow for your retirement. In addition, most children are unlikely to contribute to their parent's retirement.

This guide is designed to help alleviate these problems by showing how to plan, save, and pay for college and retirement at the same time without sacrificing current lifestyles or financial security.

When developing a funding plan for retirement and college simultaneously, long-term solutions for each funding plan are developed. When thinking only in terms of funding college, and not retirement, you may be forced to consider conservative short-term investments to meet immediate college funding needs. These conservative short-term investments may produce lower yields during college years and the years immediately proceeding the college years.

If taking a holistic long-term approach to funding college and retirement concurrently, you can invest in higher-yielding investments because of the longer time frame. You will not be forced to invest in conservative low-yielding, short-term investments for college that could have a significant negative effect on your future retirement funds.

Since there are many attractive loan programs available to you and your students to fund college, you are not forced to use conservative short-term investments or liquidate long-term investments to pay for college costs.

To make funding education and retirement a non-issue, you must consider how to:

1. Maximize cash flow in order to invest funds in education and retirement accounts.

2. Utilize the numerous education tax incentives provided by the IRS to reduce taxes and produce "tax scholarships".

3. Qualify for merit and need-based financial aid offered by colleges.

If you can maximize the benefits produced by the above strategies, you may not have to compromise your retirement and education goals.

The Education Problem

Funding education

-versus-

Sacrificing current lifestyle

Robbing retirement

At this point in time, you may be facing an education dilemma: feeling an obligation to fund your children's education, yet not wanting to sacrifice your own current lifestyle or rob your own retirement assets, in order to fund those education costs.

College is EXPENSIVE!

AVERAGE ANNUAL COST

Public University	$16,000
Average Private College	$32,000
Elite Private College	$48,000

As can be seen by the above college costs, families are faced with a big problem. How are you going to pay for college?

Historically, college costs have risen at two to three times the Consumer Price Index inflation rate.

If families are also paying for K-12 private school costs, the problem is compounded.

Now let's look at the real cost of college.

Paying for College with After-tax Dollars

Federal Tax Bracket	Public College $64,000	Private college $128,000	Elite College $192,000
25%	$91,428	$182,857	$ 274,285
28%	$95,522	$191,044	$286,567
33%	$103,225	$206,451	$309,677
35%	$92,308	$184,615	$276,923

College actually costs more than most people think because it is paid for with AFTER-TAX dollars. The numbers in this table represent what must be earned in order to pay for just one child's college education at today's prices.

Depending on which tax bracket applies, the amount that must be EARNED to pay for college is a good deal more than you may think; it is because **you must first pay the IRS, before paying the college**.

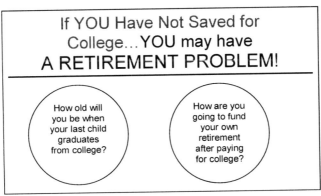

If YOU Have Not Saved for College... YOU may have A RETIREMENT PROBLEM!

How old will you be when your last child graduates from college?

How are you going to fund your own retirement after paying for college?

Another question that must be considered is..."How much will this high cost of college impede my ability to retire?"

Consider these questions:

1. How old will you be when your last child graduates from college?

2. How are you going to fund your retirement after paying for college?

3. Have you developed a financial game plan to fund these two major events?

COLLEGE $$$ SPENT
Equals
RETIREMENT $$$ LOST
Assuming an 8% Investment Rate

Number of Years Until Retirement	Public College $64,000	Private College $128,000	Elite College $192,000
15	$ 203,008	$ 406,016	$ 609,024
20	$ 298,304	$ 596,608	$ 894,912

Now consider this:

If you are 50 years old and plan to retire in 15 years, the money you invest in a four-year public college education will cost your retirement fund about $203,008, assuming an 8% return. If you have 20 years until retirement, it will cost your retirement fund $298,304. An elite private college will deplete your retirement fund by $894,912, twenty years from now. And remember, these numbers are for only one child's college education.

Because of the high cost of college, you may come up short when it comes to saving for your retirement; you may not be saving enough for retirement because you are saving or paying for your children's educational costs. Yet you, like many others, may mistakenly believe that you will be prepared for your retirement, and then may find yourself in a critical financial situation because you have saved only a fraction of what will be needed for retirement.

Since, like many parents, you may have assumed that funding your children's education is a challenge separate from funding your own retirement, you may not have realized that the real crisis facing you is a *current* cash flow problem and a *future* retirement shortfall.

The failure to recognize this fact may limit your ability to solve these problems. When families recognize college as a cash flow **and** a retirement problem, they have a longer timeframe to address these very real problems.

Many parents do not want to sacrifice their current lifestyle in order to save or pay for their children's education costs, but education costs can become a current lifestyle problem for most parents.

In summary, the challenges many parents face because of the current high cost of college are:

1. A future retirement problem.
2. A current lifestyle problem.
3. A current cash flow problem.

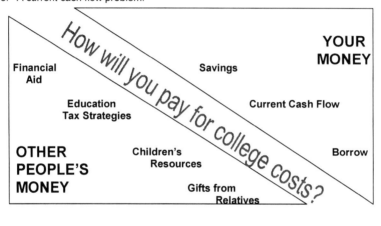

So, how do you plan to pay for college?

Actually, there are only two sources of funds:

1. **YOUR MONEY** in one of, or in a combination of, the following forms:

   - Using current cash flow

   - Using parent loans

   - Using existing savings

2. **OTHER PEOPLE'S MONEY.** This can be achieved by:

   - Using financial aid

   - Using student loans

   - Using special education tax strategies

   - Using your child's resources, i.e., their income and assets

   - Using gifts from relatives

Chapter 1
Other People's Money for College

Module 1
Financial Aid

FINANCIAL AID DEFINITION

College financial aid is money given by the federal government, the state governments, and the colleges to help students pay for the cost of a college education.

Surprisingly, a sizeable number of families who would qualify for financial aid do not apply. Why? Because they assume: "We earn too much money to qualify for aid." The result? Many families pay the full cost of college...when it isn't necessary.

Many of you will have to rely on financial aid to help pay for a portion of the cost of college. One positive aspect is that colleges and universities are more competitive than ever before in their quest for good students. Even the "prestigious" schools will compete for students from every socio-economic background. In addition, many schools have empty seats to fill and may be willing to discount their cost to fill these empty seats.

You should never assume a college is too expensive. Colleges do need paying customers; however, they do not expect *every* student and *every* family to foot the entire bill for a college education. This is especially true of private schools. All colleges have money, in the form of financial aid, and they will pay for good students.

TYPES OF FINANCIAL AID
There are two basic types of financial aid:

1. Self-help aid, which consists of interest-subsidized loans and work-study.

2. Gift aid, which consists of grants and scholarships; this money does not have to be repaid.

DETERMINING FACTORS FOR FINANCIAL AID
The amount and type of financial aid is based on two factors:

1. The **financial need of the student**. By far, this is the most important factor in determining financial aid. Most of the financial aid given by the federal and state governments is based on the financial need of the student. Also, most of the financial aid given by the colleges is need-based.

2. The **merit of the student**, i.e., scholastic, athletic, musical, etc. Any special talent or merit of a student that makes the student desirable to a college is merit.

   Note: The Ivy League colleges and other highly selective private colleges base almost all of their grants and scholarships on the financial need of the student and not the student's merit.

NEEDS ANALYSIS FORMULA

Since financial need is the most important factor in determining financial aid, let's see how it is determined. Needs analysis is the process of determining the financial need of the student. Financial need is calculated using the following formula:

	Cost of Attendance (COA)	$ 15,000
-	Expected Family Contribution (EFC)	- 7,000
=	Financial Need	8,000
-	Student Resources	- 1,000
=	Adjusted Financial Need	$ 7,000

Example: If the "cost of attendance" at a particular college is $15,000 and the "Expected Family Contribution" is calculated to be $7,000, the "financial need" of the student would be $8,000. In this case, the student would be eligible to receive $8,000 in financial aid. Whether the student receives a financial aid award for the entire $8,000 is up to the discretion of the individual college. Nonetheless, the financial aid eligibility of the student is directly related to the financial need. If the student had other "resources" to help pay for the college cost, the financial need would be reduced on a dollar-for-dollar basis for these resources. In this example, assume the student has received a $1,000 private scholarship from the local Chamber of Commerce. Since private scholarships (scholarships that are not given from the college) are considered a resource of the student, the $1,000 scholarship would reduce the financial need to $7,000. This means the student would now be eligible for only $7,000 in financial aid from the college.

If a student has no "financial need", or "adjusted financial need", the student will not be eligible for need-based financial aid. However, the student could receive merit-based scholarships.

A closer look at the individual elements of this formula is warranted to fully understand exactly how the formula works.

COST OF ATTENDANCE
Cost of attendance (COA) consists of tuition, fees, room and board, books and supplies, personal expenses, cost of a computer, and transportation to and from college. The college must furnish the COA information. Beware of this "advertised" COA: colleges may omit the cost of personal expenses and transportation expenses. The "true" COA includes the expense of travel to and from college and personal expenses, such as the student's clothing, medical and entertainment for the college year.

EXPECTED FAMILY CONTRIBUTION
Expected Family Contribution, EFC, is how much the family is expected to contribute to the total cost of college for that individual year. EFC can be thought of as the family's "college tax liability". The EFC is computed by using family financial and household data

submitted on financial aid application forms. There are two formulas that can be used to calculate the EFC. They are the Federal Methodology formula, and the Institutional Methodology formula.

Federal Methodology Formula

The Federal Methodology Formula (FM) is a federal formula used to calculate the EFC. It is used by every accredited undergraduate, graduate, and trade school in the United States to determine how much federal money can be disbursed by the school to cover the student's COA. Most states also use this formula as a basis to distribute state financial aid funds.

Institutional Methodology Formula

The Institutional Methodology Formula (IM) is an alternative formula used by some private colleges to calculate an Institutional EFC. The College Board determines this formula and makes annual changes to it.

This formula assesses the family home, the family farm, siblings' assets and other items that the Federal Methodology does not assess and is calculated prior to the disbursement of the college's own institutional funds. Since the IM takes into consideration additional factors, the EFC calculated by this method is usually higher than under the Federal Methodology.

The EFC should be calculated using both the FM and IM formulas. This is to prevent an unpleasant surprise for the family who calculates the EFC calculated using only the FM formula, and then has a student that attends a college that uses the IM formula.

The following is a simplistic version of these complex formulas:

Student's Income	-	$\begin{Bmatrix} \text{Taxes} \\ \text{\$3,000 Allowance} \end{Bmatrix}$	x 50%	Student's Contribution = from Income
				+
Student's Assets	-	$\begin{Bmatrix} \text{Nothing} \end{Bmatrix}$	x 20%	= Student's Contribution from Assets
				+
Parents' Income	-	$\begin{Bmatrix} \text{Living Allowance} \\ \text{Taxes} \end{Bmatrix}$	x 22 to 47%	Parents' Contribution = from Income
				+
Parents' Assets	-	$\begin{Bmatrix} \text{Asset Protection} \end{Bmatrix}$	x 5.6%	= Parents' Contribution from Assets
				= Expected Family Contribution

Student's Contribution

The student's income, minus taxes and a standard income protection allowance of $3,000, is assessed at a flat 50%. For example, if a student had $3,700 of income, $350 would be expected to be contributed toward the cost of college. The excess income over $3,000, which would be $700, would be assessed at a flat 50% rate to arrive at the $350 contribution.

The student's assets are assessed at a flat 20%. For example, if a student had $10,000 in a custodial account, $2,000 would be expected to be contributed toward the cost of college for that year and for each succeeding year until the account is liquidated.

Parents' Contribution

The parents' income, minus federal, social security and state taxes and a living allowance ($23,070 for a family of 4), is assessed at a graduated rate of 22% to 47%. For example, a wage bonus of $10,000 could reduce a student's eligibility for $4,700 of financial aid.

The parents' assets, minus an asset protection allowance based on the age of the older parent's age, are assessed at 5.6%. For example, if the age of the older parent were 45, the asset protection allowance would be approximately $43,000. Therefore, if the parents had assessable assets in excess of this allowance, the contribution toward college costs would be 5.6% of the excess over $43,000.

The parents' contribution, based on the above factors, is then divided by the number in the parents' household who will be enrolled in college during the same academic year.

For example, if the parents' contribution were computed to be $8,000, this amount would be divided by one if only one person in the household was planning to attend college. However, if two people in your household planned to enroll in college, your contribution would be divided by two resulting in an adjusted Parents' Contribution of only $4,000. This equates to an increase of $4,000 in financial aid eligibility for each of the two people attending college.

Caution: Since the parents' assessment rates are lower than the student's assessment rates, especially when comparing the asset assessment rates, a tax or financial planning strategy which shifts income and assets from the parents to the student may backfire when the EFC financial aid formula is considered.

Example: At the end of 2006, Albert, a parent, had the opportunity to defer $10,000 of income into 2007. His tax accountant informed him that his tax bracket would be the same for both years. Therefore, it made no difference tax-wise whether Albert paid on the income in 2006 or deferred it to 2007. However, the decision to defer or not defer the income could have a huge impact on the financial aid eligibility of his child who was a junior in high school in 2006 and would be a senior in 2007. Since Albert's 2007 income would be assessed in the financial aid formula for the child's freshman year in college, the $10,000 of additional income in 2006 could cause a potential financial aid loss of $4,700 (47% x $10,000) for the child. Therefore, the decision to defer or not defer income should not be made solely based on income tax planning, but also needs to include financial aid planning.

Example: A tax accountant was approached by a parent who wanted to be able to deduct some of the college expenses the parent was about to incur for his child, a senior in high school. Since the parent owned a sole-proprietor business, the accountant recommended that the parent pay his child $6,500 for work performed during the summer and on college breaks. The child could use the wages to pay for upcoming *college costs. Therefore, the parent was indirectly receiving a tax deduction for the college costs. In this scenario, the child could possibly lose $1,750 in financial aid ($6,500 - $3,000 allowance x 50%). A large portion of the $1,750 loss could consist of grant or scholarship aid. A family should always consider both the tax and financial aid ramifications of any income shifting strategy.*

DATES OF ASSESSMENT

Incomes of the parents and the student are assessed using year-end data from the year, commonly called the "base year", prior to the year when the student will be entering college. For the 2007-2008 college year, income will be assessed using the 2006 calendar year information, e.g., 2006 tax return.

Assets of the parents and the student are assessed as of the date the financial aid application forms are signed.

Planning tip: Since a student will file the final financial aid application form in the spring of the junior year in college, the income the student makes in that calendar year will not affect the student's eligibility for financial aid. Therefore, the student can have unlimited income during that calendar year without a reduction in financial aid eligibility. It may be a tax benefit for the student's parents or grandparents to shift income to the student during this period.

Example: On January 15, 2007, Judy, a college junior, filed her financial aid application form for her senior year in college. Her financial aid eligibility for her senior year in college is based on her income for the calendar year 2006. In the summer of 2007, she received a gift of highly appreciated stock from her parents. She sold the stock and reported a capital gain of $18,000 on her 2007 income tax return. Since the income was reported in 2007, the income had no effect on her financial aid eligibility and the family tax savings was $1,800 ($2,700 capital gain tax if reported by her parents minus $900 actually paid on her tax return).

QUALIFYING PARAMETERS

To get a rough estimate of the EFC produced by various combinations of income and assets, refer to the following table.

Note: In the table, note the drastic drop in EFC (the EFC is on a per student basis) when there are two members of the family in college. Also note that if the COA at a particular college is less than the EFC shown in the table, the child will not be eligible to receive need-based financial aid at that particular college.

QUALIFYING PARAMETERS*								
Parents' Income	$50,000	$75,000	$100,000	$100,000	$150,000	$150,000	$200,000	$200,000
Assets	$50,000	$75,000	$100,000	$100,000	$100,000	$200,000	$100,000	$100,000
Number in College	1	1	1	2	1	1	1	2
Number in Family	5	5	5	5	5	5	5	5
EFC per Student	$3,300	$9,500	$20,200	$10,100	$39,700	$45,300	$53,800	$26,900

- This table assumes the student has income of less than $3,000 and there are no assets in the student's name.

Caution: You should not assume that if you do not appear to qualify for financial aid based on the above table that you will not qualify for financial aid. Future events, such as death, disability, divorce, unemployment or natural disasters, may make you eligible for financial aid. Also, if the student qualifies as an "independent student", the income and assets of the parents are not considered in the EFC calculation.

FINANCIAL NEED

Financial Need is the total amount of financial aid that the student is eligible to receive. The total amount of financial aid received by the student usually will not exceed the financial need of the student. When analyzing the student's need, some colleges will meet 100% of the student's total financial need, and other colleges will meet only a percentage of the student's total need. Private colleges tend to fill the financial need with a higher percentage of gift aid than do public colleges. The private colleges do this to put their cost on a level playing field with the cost of public colleges in order to attract good students.

PUBLIC VS. PRIVATE COLLEGE

Public University		**Private College**	
Cost	$ 16,000	Cost	$ 32,000
EFC	- 5,000	EFC	- 5,000
NEED	$ 11,000	NEED	$ 27,000
% Need Met	80%	% Need Met	100%
Financial Aid:	$ 8,800	Financial Aid:	$ 27,000
Gift Aid (20%)	$ 1,760	Gift Aid (70%)	$ 18,900
Self Help (80%)	$ 7,040	Self Help (30%)	$ 8,100
"Out-of-Pocket Cost"	$ 7,200	"Out-of-Pocket Cost"	$ 5,000
(Cost - Financial Aid)		(Cost - Financial Aid)	
"True Cost"	**$ 14,240**	**"True Cost"**	**$13,100**
(Cost - Gift Aid)		(Total Cost - Gift Aid)	

11

The preceding comparison illustrates how a typical public and private college will fill the financial need of a student. Notice that the "true cost" of a private college is considerably less than its published "sticker price."

STUDENT RESOURCES

"Student Resources" are sources of funding outside the family's income and assets, which the student has available and the college feels the student can use to pay for college. Colleges will lower the financial need of the student on a dollar-for-dollar basis for the amount of any resource of the student. Some common types of student resources are:

1. Private scholarships or grants received by business or fraternal organizations

2. Veterans Educational, VA, benefits received from the federal government

3. Cash gifts paid directly to the college for tuition from outside the immediate family, such as college tuition paid by grandparents

4. Employer-provided education assistance programs received from the student's employer

5. Any other funds that the college feels the student has at their disposal to pay for college, such as ROTC assistance, scholarships and subsistence, Veterans/VEAP/Reserve or Guard benefits, or Vocational Rehabilitation benefits

NON-ASSESSABLE ASSETS
There are certain non-assessable assets that do not have to be reported on financial aid application forms, and therefore, will not affect the EFC. These items are as follows:

Annuities
Annuities (including both qualified and non-qualified annuities) are non-assessable assets.

> **Observation:** Some private colleges do assess annuities when computing the EFC. You or your financial advisor should contact each college that the student is interested in attending and inquire about its policy regarding assessment of annuities.

Life Insurance
Life insurance cash value is not assessed.

> **Observation:** Some private colleges do assess life insurance cash value when computing the EFC. You or your financial advisor should contact each college that the student is interested in attending and inquire about its policy regarding assessment of life insurance.

Retirement Accounts
Retirement accounts, such as a 401(k), 403(b), IRA, SEP, and Keogh, are non-assessable assets. The Roth IRA is also not assessed.

> **Note:** A Coverdell Education Savings Account (CESA), formerly known as an Education IRA, is considered an asset of the parent and is assessed at the parents' asset assessment rate.

Personal Items
Personal items such as cars, clothes, and household items are not assessed. Debt corresponding to personal items cannot be listed on the financial aid application forms.

Personal Residence
The family's personal residence is a non-assessable asset; however, second or vacation homes are assessable assets. Note, the IM formula will assess the net worth of a personal residence.

Family Farm/Business
The family farm or business is a non-assessable asset. A family farm is defined as the family's principal place of residence and the family operates the farm. The family business is defines as a business where the family has significant ownership interest and materially participates in its operation. The business must have less than 100 full-time employees The IM formula will assess the net worth of a family farm or business.

A farm that does not meet the criteria for a family farm is considered an "investment farm" and must be reported at its current market value.

Siblings' Assets
The assets of the student's siblings are not assessed under the FM. However, the siblings' assets, including assets in a Coverdell Education Savings Account or a Qualified Tuition Plan, commonly called 529 Plans, will be assessed under the IM Formula. These assets are assessed as parental assets at a 5.6% rate.

QUALIFIED TUITION PLANS
Qualified Tuition Plans (QTPs) commonly called 529 Plans, are state-sponsored trusts used to save for future tuition, related fees, and room and board costs at a particular university system or college.

There are two basic types of QTPs, the "prepaid tuition plan" and the "college savings plan."

Prepaid Tuition Plans
These state-operated trusts offer residents a hedge against tuition inflation. States offer contracts whereby they agree to pay future tuition at in-state public institutions at prices pegged to current tuition levels. Some state contracts incorporate a further discount derived from a share of the program trust fund's projected future investment gains in excess of anticipated tuition increases.

Prepaid Tuition Plans are assessable assets. The IM formula assesses prepaid tuition plans as assets of the parent, regardless of who owns the account. Prepaid tuition plans held in the student's siblings' names will be also assessed as a parental asset at a rate of 5.6% under the IM formula.

College Savings Plans
Essentially a state-sponsored mutual fund, the basic idea of a savings plan is that the account owner's contribution will grow in value over time, keeping up with or surpassing the escalating price of a college education.

> **Note:** Website information for tuition prepayment, or savings plans, can be found at: www.savingforcollege.com.

College savings plans are assessed as an asset of the parent at a rate of 5.6%, if the parent is the owner of the plan.

If a person other than the student or the student's parent owns the plan, such as a grandparent, it is not assessed in the EFC formulas.

If a trust or custodial account of the student is the owner of the plan, the assets of the plan are assessed as a parent's asset.

The earning's portion of distributions from the QTP is not assessed as income of the student; the principal portion withdrawn has no impact on college financial aid.

Under the IM formula, college savings plans are treated as an asset of the parents if either the student or parent owns the account.

TRUST AND CUSTODIAL ACCOUNTS
Trust and Uniform Gift to Minors Act, UGMA, or Uniform Transfer to Minors Act, UTMA, and assets should be reported on the financial aid application at their present value, even if the beneficiary's access to the trust is restricted. Trust assets do not have to be reported when they are restricted by court order for a specific purpose (e.g., future medical expenses of an accident victim).

There may be some adverse legal and tax consequences to pulling assets out of a trust or UGMA/UTMA and putting them in another person's name. It may be illegal to take money out of a trust account and not use it for the benefit of the beneficiary. The transfer of money out of a trust may be considered taxable income to the person receiving the money. These consequences must be investigated before transferring money.

NON-ASSESSABLE INCOME

There are certain types of non-assessable income that does not have to be reported on the financial aid application forms and therefore will not affect the EFC. These items are as follows:

EMPLOYER PROVIDED EDUCATION ASSISTANCE BENEFITS
Education Assistance Benefits received from an employer are not reportable on an employee's financial aid application. However, the amount of the benefit is considered a

"resource" and reduces the financial need of the student on a dollar-for-dollar basis.

LOAN PROCEEDS
Loan proceeds from any source are not assessed. This would include loans from life insurance, retirement accounts, residences, student loans, etc.

"ROLLOVER" PENSIONS
The portion of a pension withdrawal, which is not "rolled over" to another type of pension, is assessed; however, any rollover portion is not assessed. For example, if you roll your 401(k) to an IRA it is a non-assessable rollover.

GIFTS AND SUPPORT
Gifts and support, other than money, received from friends or relatives are not assessed. Therefore, cash gifts are considered financial aid income and are assessed.

Non-monetary gifts, such as stocks or automobiles, are not assessed.

VETERANS EDUCATIONAL BENEFITS
Veterans Administration (VA) educational benefits, including VA work-study, are not assessed. However, the amount of the benefit is considered a "resource" and reduces the financial need of the student on a dollar-for-dollar basis.

FLEXIBLE SPENDING PLAN CONTRIBUTIONS
Contributions to, or payments from, flexible spending plans, e.g., cafeteria plans, are not assessed in the FM formula. This includes Medical Savings Accounts (MSA) and Health Savings Accounts (HAS). The IM formula does assess contributions to these accounts.

Flexible spending plans increase a student's financial aid eligibility as they reduce the parents' income.

> *Example: Parents who contributed $8,000 to their flexible spending plans for dependent care and medical expenses reduced their income by the $8,000. This reduction increased their child's financial aid eligibility because the parents' income was reduced by this amount.*

FINANCIAL AID INCOME AND BENEFITS

There are numerous "Untaxed Income and Benefits" which are considered financial aid income.

UNTAXED INCOME AND BENEFITS

Current Year Retirement Contributions
Deductible IRA, SIMPLE IRA, SEP or Keogh contributions for the current year are assessed. In addition, payments to tax-deferred pension and savings plans are assessed. This includes the current contributions to 401(k) and 403(b) plans.

Example: A student's parent made a $3,000 tax-deductible contribution to a regular IRA. The $3,000 is considered an "untaxed benefit" and is used in the EFC computations.

Untaxed Portion of Retirement Withdrawal

Untaxed portions of retirement, pension, annuities, or life insurance withdrawals, excluding loans, are assessed. This includes distributions from Roth IRAs, whether taxable or non-taxable.

The taxable conversion of a regular IRA to a Roth IRA causes an increase in income. Therefore, parents need to consider the financial aid effect that this conversion has on their children who will be attending college during the conversion year.

If a child qualifies for financial aid, avoid withdrawals from the types of investments described in this section during college years.

Living Allowance

Housing, food, and other living allowances, excluding rent subsidies for low-income housing, paid to members of the military, clergy, and others, including cash payments and cash value benefits, as compensation for their jobs are assessed, e.g., if a family receives the tax-free use of an apartment, the rental value of the apartment would be reported. Housing allowances excludes rent subsidies for low-income housing.

Example: Room and board provided as a non-taxable fringe benefit by a corporation for its employees would be considered an "untaxed benefit."

Untaxed Portions of Social Security Benefits

If Social Security benefits are paid to parents on behalf of a student, because the student was under 18 years old at the time, those benefits are reported as the parents' income, not the student's. If the Social Security benefits are payable to the student, they are reported as the student's income.

Planning tip: If a family is currently receiving Social Security benefits that will end during an upcoming college year, the family should appeal this situation to the college. The basis of the appeal would be that the payments will end during the college year and the family will not have these funds available to pay for college.

Child Support Payments

Child support payments received for all the parents' children are assessed.

Planning tip: A divorce or separation could be structured to give the custodial parent more assets and smaller child support payments. The custodial parent's assets would be assessed at 5.6% versus the maximum financial aid income assessment rate of 47%.

Income Exclusions

Income exclusions, such as the exclusion of the gain on the sale of a personal residence, are assessed. Even though these items are not taxable, they must be reported as "untaxed income," as they represent additional financial funds available to the family.

FINANCIAL AID INCOME DEDUCTIONS
There are certain items that are deducted from financial aid income:

Child Support Paid
Child support paid by the parents or student is a deduction in calculating the EFC.

Need-based Work Programs
Federal work-study or other need-based work programs can be deducted if they were included in the student's taxable income.

This deduction is often missed by financial advisors and families. Work-study can often be identified on a W-2 issued to the student by the college or university because it is exempt from Social Security tax.

Taxable Grants and Scholarships
Taxable grant and scholarship aid that is included in the student's taxable income is a deduction against the student's income.

Federal Income Tax
Federal income tax paid, actual tax paid, not the amount withheld, is a deduction. This does not include the Alternative Minimum Tax, AMT, Social Security tax on tips, the 10% penalty on early withdrawals from retirement accounts, the advance earned income credit, or household employment taxes.

State Tax Allowance
An allowance for state tax is a deduction. This is automatically calculated by the financial aid processing center in the financial aid formula, based on the state of residency.

Social Security Tax
Social Security tax paid is a deduction. This is automatically calculated by the financial aid processing center based on the amount of earned income of the parents and student.

Living Allowance or Income Protection Allowance
In the parents' case, this is automatically calculated in the financial aid formula based on the number of household members and the number of college students in the household. The following table will give you an idea of the amount of the parents' Living Allowance or Income Protection Allowance.

PARENT'S LIVING ALLOWANCE TABLE					
Number in parents' household, including student	NUMBER OF COLLEGE STUDENTS IN HOUSEHOLD				
	1	2	3	4	5
2	$ 15,000	$ 12,430			
3	$ 18,680	$ 16,130	$ 13,560		
4	$ 23,070	$ 20,510	$ 17,950	$ 15,390	
5	$ 27,220	$ 24,660	$ 22,100	$ 19,540	$ 16,980
6	$ 31,840	$ 29,280	$ 26,770	$ 24,100	$ 21,600

In the student's case, the Living Allowance is a fixed standard allowance. For the college year 2007-2008, the allowance is $3,000 for the Federal Methodology EFC formula. The Institutional Methodology EFC formula does not allow a Living Allowance against the student's income.

Employment Expense Allowance
This is automatically calculated by the financial aid processing centers by multiplying the lesser of the earned income of the father or mother times 35%. The maximum allowance for 2007-2008 is $3,200.

> **Planning Tip**: In order to qualify for this allowance, families with closely-held businesses can enable a parent, who does not have earned income, to receive earned income from the business.

MERIT BASED FINANCIAL AID

Most colleges will award merit-based scholarships dependent on the student's talent. These scholarships are awarded regardless of the financial need of the student.

In addition, many private colleges have empty seats to fill. To fill these empty seats, they may offer a discount on their tuition. These tuition discounts come in the form of grants and scholarships.

To increase your child's chances of receiving merit aid, you should try to create competition for your child by having him/her apply to many colleges.

You should also take advantage of the colleges' desire to achieve cultural diversity within their student body. If your child has qualities that would add to the cultural diversity at a college, the college should be informed of these qualities.

MERIT SCHOLARSHIPS
It is important to ask the college for information on merit scholarships and other merit incentives, as they differ from college to college. Students wishing to be considered for these scholarships must correctly position themselves to receive these scholarships.

Proper positioning begins early in high school and involves the following three factors:

Good grades in challenging courses
Good grades are self-explanatory. Colleges assume that good grades in high school will lead to good grades in college and a better graduation rate for their enrollees. A student should receive a minimum GPA of 3.0 in high school to be considered for merit awards and tuition discounts.

Good SAT/ACT test scores
The SAT/ACT college prep tests are the only standard measure colleges have when comparing the academic abilities of a student in Kansas with a student in Florida. To have a good chance at getting merit awards or tuition discounts, a student should have a minimum of a 24 ACT or 1250 SAT (verbal and math) score.

A solid resume of achievement
Students should build a strong resume of achievement throughout their high school years. This includes extra-curricular activities and clubs, as well as civic groups or community service projects the student is involved in. This will demonstrate to the college that the student has many abilities and interests outside the classroom. The student should send a résumé with the admission application to each school.

TUITION DISCOUNTS
Many private colleges offer tuition discounts to stay competitive with the lower-cost state universities and competing private colleges. Regardless of the student's qualifications for need-based financial aid, private colleges will discount their "sticker price" to help attract students. Students should always apply to private colleges to determine if they qualify for these tuition discounts.

In order to increase the chances of receiving a tuition discount, the student should apply to the selected private colleges early in the senior year of high school, September thru December. The rule of thumb is the earlier the better! Remember, once a college begins to fill the upcoming year's freshman class, the need for the college to offer a tuition discount diminishes.

The student should apply to a minimum of six colleges. Applying to several colleges gives the student the opportunity to receive a tuition discount from one college and use that discount to ask for a comparative discount, or better, from the college the student prefers to attend.
The student should attempt to create competition among the selected colleges for the student. In order to create competition, the following factors should be considered:

1. The student should apply to colleges that are competitive in the same area or location, athletic conference, or intellectual fields. Private colleges are more likely to give a significant tuition discount if they know the student is also applying to one of their competitor schools. Many times the most competition occurs between colleges that are in the same athletic conference.

2. The student should always apply to a good in-state public university. The public university's low "sticker price" may force the private college to offer a tuition discount

to make its cost competitive with the public university's cost. Low-cost public universities are the private colleges' main competition for students.

3. The student should apply to similar private colleges that are located outside of the student's region of residency. Most private colleges try to achieve regional diversity in their student bodies. In an attempt to accomplish this, the college may offer tuition discounts to entice students that are coming from a different region.

4. The student should apply to private colleges where the student may add to the cultural diversity at these colleges. Most private colleges try to achieve cultural diversity in their student bodies. In an attempt to accomplish this, the college may offer tuition discounts to entice students that will add to the cultural diversity of the student body.

5. The student should apply to private colleges that have declining enrollments. Many private colleges have declining enrollments due to their high costs and competition from low-cost public universities and popular elite private colleges. Many times these colleges will give a tuition discount to the student to fill an empty seat at the college.

6. The student should apply to colleges that have a high amount of students that are admitted, but a lower number that actually enroll, known as a low "enrollment yield". The lower a college's enrollment yield, the higher the probability of the student receiving tuition discounts.

7. The student should apply to colleges where the student is academically above the incoming freshman class profile. Private colleges place a premium on good students and will often use tuition discounts to attract them to their campuses. In order to help the student obtain a tuition discount from the financial aid office, they may enlist the college admission's officer or other college officials, such as a departmental head or coach.

PRIVATE SCHOLARSHIPS
Even though the private sector produces only 1% of the available college financial aid, you still should pursue every possible source of monies to reduce your college costs.

Most of these private monies available are from local organizations and companies. Very few national awards fit a particular student. The student's high school guidance counselor will generally be aware of local scholarships, and can help the student identify those that match the student's qualifications. Also, you should check for scholarship offerings by the various memberships and product relationships used by your family. For example, if the family is a member of any fraternal insurance organizations, those entities will often offer scholarships to members or to children of members. Similarly, you household insurance provider, local utility company, or similar entities may offer scholarships to customers.

You should be aware that there are scholarship search companies that charge a fee for a scholarship search. Many of these companies scam families.

APPEALING A FINANCIAL AID AWARD

APPEAL PROCESS

When a college's award letter does not meet the student's financial needs, either in the total amount of aid or in the type of aid, the student can appeal the award to the college. Most colleges have an appeal process that allows students to request a review of their financial aid eligibility and corresponding financial aid award offer. Each college determines its own regulations for this process, and students should be aware of a particular college's procedures.

> **Planning tip:** If the student does appeal an award letter, the student should be specific in requesting additional funds. The student should clearly state the reasons for the appeal, and request a specific amount of money. The student should write the request and submit any required documents with the letter of appeal. Then the student should contact the college's financial aid administrator, FAA. It is preferable that the contact be made in person; if this is not possible, the contact should be made by a telephone call. The "personal touch" is important to a successful appeal.

PROFESSIONAL JUDGMENT

In the appeal letter, the student should ask the Financial Aid Administrator, FAA, to exercise "Professional Judgment." Professional Judgment is the authority given to the college FAA to change the family's financial and household data in any way that would more accurately measure the family's ability to pay for educational costs. If the student is to successfully appeal an award letter, the student must fully understand the concept and definition of Professional Judgment. Professional Judgment may only be made in special circumstances, and only when the family provides adequate documentation of these special circumstances.

SPECIAL CIRCUMSTANCES

Special circumstances are not limited to elementary and high school tuition, unusual medical or dental expenses, dislocated worker, unemployed worker, or unusually high childcare expenses. It could include circumstances that were considered to be "special conditions", such as divorce, separation, or the death of a parent or spouse after the application was filed. If these situations occur, the college's FAA must be contacted to see if the aid award can be increased.

Professional Judgment can also be used by the FAA in other situations as follows:

1. Adjust the college cost of attendance to take into account special circumstances such as medical needs or excessive travel costs.

2. Override the student's dependency status to make a "dependent student" an "independent student".

3. Adjust the income and assets of a family located in a federally declared natural disaster area.

Example: A family, residing in a county that was declared a Federal Natural Disaster Area due to flooding, appealed the income and asset amounts reported on the FAFSA to the FAA at the college their child was attending. The family documented that the value of the building, which contained the family business, had been greatly reduced due to damage sustained during the flood. The family did not have flood insurance to cover the damage. Also, the family's income generated by the business assets would be greatly reduced during the upcoming period of clean up and repair. The FAA agreed that this was indeed a special circumstance and adjusted the student's original FAFSA amounts and increased the amount of the original financial aid award.

4. Any other "special circumstance" that the family and/or its financial advisor can convince the FAA to adjust the EFC data elements.

Example: A parent was able to convince the FAA that his "un-reimbursed business expenses," should reduce his income because they were actually "out-of-pocket" expenses against his income.

Example: A parent was able to convince the FAA that the bonus he received from his employer was a one-time event and that it distorted his normal income level.

Example: Parents convinced the FAA that their income and expenses did not clearly indicate their ability to contribute to their child's college education. The parents showed the FAA that their income was inflated due to a required retirement withdrawal for a parent who had been recently released from his job. They also proved to the FAA that they had excessive medical bills for a handicapped sibling.

Example: A student convinced the FAA that his employment income would be much less during college years than was reported on the FAFSA.

Planning tip: The appeal of an award letter has a much greater chance of success if the student has the type of merit, such as academic, athletic, musical, etc., that the college needs to fill its enrollment needs. In the appeal letter, the merit of the student should be emphasized to the FAA. This is especially true at private colleges that seek to attract students with merit.

Module 2
Student Loans for College

TYPES OF STUDENT LOANS

NEED-BASED:
- **Federal Subsidized Stafford Loan**
- **Federal Perkins Loan**

NON-NEED BASED:
- **College Loan**
- **Federal Unsubsidized Stafford Loan**
- **State Loans**
- **Private Loans**
- **Intra-family Loans**

In this section we will explore loan options that the student has available to fund college costs. There are need-based loans that require that the student demonstrate financial need to qualify for the loans. In addition, there are non-need based loans that do not require the student to demonstrate their financial need.

NEED-BASED STUDENT LOANS

FEDERAL SUBSIDIZED STAFFORD LOANS
Federal Subsidized Stafford Loans are fixed-rate, need-based loans varying from $3,500 for college freshman, $4,500 for sophomores, and $5,500 for juniors and higher. The interest is paid or subsidized, by the federal government until six months after the student leaves college and the interest rate on the repayment is capped at 8.25%. Stafford Loans carry both life and disability insurance on the student. If the student dies or becomes disabled, the loan balance is forgiven.

FEDERAL PERKINS LOANS
Federal Perkins Loans are low-interest, need-based loans ranging up to $4,000 per year. The interest, whose rate is fixed at 5%, is subsidized by the federal government until six months after the student leaves college. The college determines which students will receive this loan and the amount of the loan.

NON-NEED BASED STUDENT LOANS

COLLEGE LOANS
Some colleges have student loan programs that may or may not be based on the financial need of the student. The terms and rate of these loans vary with each

individual college. You should inquire to the college about the availability of loan programs through the college.

FEDERAL UNSUBSIDIZED STAFFORD LOANS
Unsubsidized Stafford Loans are not need-based loans. If there is no financial need, the student can still receive an Unsubsidized Stafford Loan, which is subject to the Subsidized Stafford Loan limits. The interest rate and repayment terms are the same as the Federal Subsidized Stafford Loan. The interest is not subsidized by the federal government during the time the student is in college. However, repayment of these loans will not start until six months after the student leaves college.

STATE LOANS
Some states have college loan programs. State loan programs may or may not be based on the financial need of the student. The state's Higher Education Agency can provide the details of its loan programs.

PRIVATE LOANS
There are loans from private sources that can provide supplemental educational financing for undergraduate and graduate students.

Following are some sources of private loans:

1. College Funding Company (1-800-745-6646)

2. Educaid (1-800-EDUCAID)

3. Educap (1-800-230-4080)

4. First of America (1-800-322-2212)

5. GATE Student Loan Program (www.gateloan.com)

6. Key Education Resources (www.key.com/educate)

7. Massachusetts Educational Financing Authority (1-800-449-MEFA)

8. MedFunds (1-800-665-1016)

9. Nellie Mae LOAN LINK (www.nelliemae.com)

10. TERI Alternative Loan Program (1-800-255-8374)

11. TERI Continuing Education Loan (www.teri.org)

12. Chela Financial (www.chelafin.com)

13. Citibank (www.citibank.com)

14. Connecticut Student Loan Foundation (www.cslf.com)

15. Sallie Mae (www.salliemae.com)

16. Southwest Student Service Corporation (www.sssc.com)

17. Bank of America (www.bankofamerica.com)

18. Wells Fargo Bank (www.wellsfargo.com)

19. PLATO (www.plato.org)

20. U.S. Bank (www.estudentloan.com)

Note: Sallie Mae has a student loan program called the "Signature Student Loan." These loans are in the student's name, but the parents may have to co-sign the loan. A co-borrower may be required if the student is a freshman, or has no credit history or a low credit rating.

These signature loans can be repaid over a period of up to 25 years and repayment doesn't start until 6 months after graduation. After the student makes 24 on-time payments, the co-borrower can be removed from the loan. A student can borrow up to $25,000 per year without a co-borrower, and up to $35,000 per year with a co-borrower. The maximum any one student can borrow is $100,000.

INTRA-FAMILY LOANS

Generally, a disparity exists between the rate of earnings on an investment and the interest rate a borrower must pay on a loan. Loaning money to a child for college costs can offer savings opportunities for both the parents and the child. The parents may be able to both increase their rate of return on investments and assist their child in paying for college. The child may increase cash flow for college, due to the lower interest rate on the loan than could be obtained from other financing.

Example: The parents have $150,000 in their savings account that earns 3% annually. Their child needs $125,000 for college; however, the 7% interest rate the child needs to pay to a lending institution is higher than the child would like to pay. The parents want to loan the student the money, however, they need the income generated from their savings account to live on. The parties agree on a 5% interest rate on the loan. The parents' income tax rate is 28%. In this case, the parents will have an increase in earnings of $2,500 [(5% - 3%) x $125,000], less the increased tax liability of $700, or a net after-tax increase to cash flow of $1,800. The student will have a decrease in interest expense of $2,500 [(7% - 5%) x $125,000]. The combined increase in family cash flow is $4,300 ($1,800 + $2,500).

Note: The interest paid on loans from relatives is not deductible as student loan interest expense.

Module 3
Education Tax Incentives

In this section we will explore education tax incentives that can reduce a family's income tax liability. The tax savings can be used to help fund college costs.

HOPE SCHOLARSHIP CREDIT, HC

The Hope Scholarship Credit (HC) is a non-refundable credit against an individual's federal income tax liability.

CALCULATION OF CREDIT
The HC is calculated by taking 100% of the first $1,100 of "qualified tuition and related expenses" plus 50% of the excess of these expenses up to a $1,100 limit.

> *Example: If the qualified expenses of an individual student were $3,500, the HC would be $1,650 (100% x $1,100 plus 50% x $1,100). If the expenses were only $1,600, the HC would be $1,350 (100% x $1,100 plus 50% x $500).*

MAXIMUM CREDIT ALLOWED
The maximum HC allowed per student is $1,650 per year. The credit can be claimed for each student claimed on the parents' tax return.

For example, if there are two "eligible students" who have qualified expenses, a maximum HC of $3,300 (2 students x $1,650) can be claimed.

CREDIT PHASE-OUT
The HC is phased-out when the taxpayer reaches certain levels of "Modified Adjusted Gross Income." The credit is ratably phased out for modified AGI of between $45,000 to $55,000 for single and head of household taxpayers; and between $90,000 to $110,000 for married taxpayers; for 2006.

> *Example: A married taxpayer with $100,000 in modified AGI would have a maximum HC of $825 per eligible student.*

> **Planning tip:** As a tax planning strategy, families who have Modified AGI in excess of the phase-out levels (Single—$55,000 or Married—$110,000) may not want to claim the student as a dependent. The student can claim the HC, provided the student's Modified AGI is not above the phase-out limits.

> *Example: Ken, the parent, elects not to claim his daughter, Linda, as a dependent on his tax return, even though he is eligible to do so by reason of having provided over 50% of her support for the year. Under IRS regulations, Linda is now eligible to claim the Hope Credit on her Federal income tax return, and Ken is not allowed to claim any education credit. This same result occurs whether the parent or the child actually pays the qualified tuition.*

Assume that Linda has $5,000 of ordinary income during 2006 from wages, interest, and dividends, and $13,000 of long-term capital gain from stock sales and mutual fund distributions. Further, assume there was at least $2,200 of tuition paid in 2006 that is eligible for the Hope Credit. By declining to claim Linda's exemption on the parental return, a $643 Hope Credit will be recognized on her return, calculated as follows:

LINDA'S 2006 FORM 1040

Wages, interest & dividend income	$ 5,000
Capital gain on stock/fund sales	13,000
AGI	18,000
Less 2006 standard deduction	- 5,150
Taxable income	$ 12,850

Tax:

5% on $12,850	643
Income tax	643
Less Hope Credit ($1,650 limit)	- 643
Net tax	$ -0-

QUALIFIED EXPENSES

The HC is only available for certain qualified expenses for undergraduate courses at "eligible educational institutions." Qualified expenses are tuition and related fees at these eligible educational institutions, and do not include books, room and board, personal transportation or living expenses, activity fees, or insurance. The qualified expenses have to actually be paid during the academic period or, if paid in a prior tax year the academic period must begin within the first three months of the next year.

The qualified expenses are reduced by tax-free grants or scholarships, employer provided educational assistance, veteran's education benefits, tax-free withdrawals from a Qualified Tuition Plan or Coverdell Education Savings Account, and qualified expenses deducted elsewhere on the tax return.

Only out-of-pocket qualified expenses are used to calculate the HC. The expenses may be paid by the student, the parents of the student or by a third party, such as a grandparent, for the student. The expenses can be paid, with no reduction in qualified expenses, by loans, savings, savings from a qualified tuition program, gifts, bequests, devises, or inheritances.

Note: Loan repayments for qualified expenses do not count as qualified expenses in calculating the HC.

Example: Harry has enrolled in a post secondary vocational program that requires $1,500 of tuition in September of 2007. Harry's second semester of this program begins February 3, 2008, and again requires about $1,500 of tuition, due by January 31, 2008. To maximize the 2007 Hope Credit, Harry's parents are permitted to prepay tuition in

December of 2007 for the academic period beginning in February 2008. Accordingly, Harry's parents should prepay $700 of tuition in December of 2007 to qualify for the full $1,650 Hope Credit in their 2007 Form 1040.

If a third party, defined as someone other than the taxpayer, taxpayer's spouse, or a claimed dependent, makes a payment **directly** to the educational institution to pay tuition, the tuition is treated as paid by the student for purposes of the credits.

ELIGIBLE STUDENTS
The student must be enrolled in a degree, certificate, or other program leading to a recognized educational credential at an eligible educational institution; this includes an approved program of study abroad. The student must be enrolled on at least a half-time basis, which is usually 6 credits.

The student must not have been convicted of a federal or state drug felony offense consisting of the possession or distribution of a controlled substance to be eligible for the HC.

LIFETIME LEARNING CREDIT, LC

The Lifetime Learning Credit, LC, is a non-refundable credit against the individual's federal income tax liability.

CALCULATION OF CREDIT
The LC is calculated by taking 20% of up to a maximum of $10,000 in "qualified tuition and related expenses." The limit for the LC is $2,000 per taxpayer tax return.

> *Example: If a family has a combined total of $12,000 in qualified tuition expenses for all the exemptions claimed on the tax return, the LC for the tax return would be $2,000, 20% x $10,000 maximum qualified expenses. If the same family only had combined expenses of $8,000, the LC would be $1,600, 20% x $8,000.*

MAXIMUM CREDIT ALLOWED
The maximum LC allowed is $2,000 per taxpayer return, **not** per eligible student. The qualified expenses for all eligible students can be combined to reach the maximum credit of $2,000.

> *Example: If there are two eligible students and each has qualified expenses of $10,000, the maximum LC that could be claimed is $2,000 per that taxpayer return.*

CREDIT PHASE-OUT
The LC is phased out when the taxpayer reaches certain levels: $45,000 to $55,000, for single or head-of-household; and $90,000 - $110,000 for married taxpayers; of the modified AGI.

> *A married taxpayer, with $100,000 modified AGI, would have a maximum LC of $1,000.*

Planning tip: As a tax planning strategy, families who have a modified AGI in excess of the phase-out levels: single or head of household, $55,000; or married taxpayers, $110,000; may want to give up the student as a tax exemption. The student can then claim the LC, provided the student's Modified AGI is not also above the phase-out limits.

Planning tip: Another tax planning strategy to consider for families with two students in college at the same time, is for the parents to give up one of the students as a tax exemption. This student can then claim the LC for the expenses on their tax return, provided the student's modified AGI is not above the phase-out limits. In addition, the other student's qualified expenses could be claimed for the LC on the parents' tax return, provided the parents' modified AGI is not above the phase-out limits. The overall result of this strategy would be that two LCs, instead of only one LC, could be claimed by this family on the two separate taxpayer returns.

QUALIFIED EXPENSES

The LC is available for certain qualified expenses for undergraduate, graduate, or professional degree courses at eligible educational institutions. Qualified expenses are the same as for the HC and are tuition and related fees at these eligible educational institutions, but do not include books, room and board, personal transportation or living expenses, activity fees, or insurance. The qualified expenses have to actually be paid during the academic period or, if paid in a prior tax year the academic period must begin within the first three months of the next year.

The qualified expenses are reduced by tax-free grants or scholarships, employer provided educational assistance, veterans' education benefits, tax-free withdrawals from a Qualified Tuition Plan or Coverdell Education Savings Account, and qualified expenses deducted elsewhere on the tax return.

Only out-of-pocket qualified expenses are used to calculate the LC. The expenses may be paid by the student, the parents of the student or by a third party, such as a grandparent, for the student. The expenses can be paid, with no reduction in qualified expenses, by loans, savings, savings from a qualified tuition program, gifts, bequests, devises, or inheritances.

> **Note:** Loan repayments for qualified expenses do not count as qualified expenses in calculating the LC.

If a third party, defined as someone other than the taxpayer, taxpayer's spouse, or a claimed dependent, makes a payment **directly** to the educational institution to pay tuition, the tuition is treated as paid by the student for purposes of the credits.

ELIGIBLE STUDENTS

There is no limit to the number of years in which an eligible student may claim the LC. The student must be the taxpayer, the taxpayer's spouse, or a dependent of the taxpayer.

The definition of an eligible student is the same as in the HC, with three exceptions:

1.   The student may be enrolled less than half-time and still qualify for the LC;

2.   The courses, at eligible educational institutions, taken by the student are allowed to be taken to acquire or improve job skills; and

3.   The student convicted of a federal or state drug felony can qualify for the LC.

PENALTY-FREE IRA WITHDRAWALS

Penalty-free withdrawals from regular IRAs can be made to pay for undergraduate or graduate, qualified higher education expenses for the taxpayer, the taxpayer's spouse, or the child or grandchild of the taxpayer or taxpayer's spouse at an eligible educational institution. The taxpayer will owe federal income tax on the amount withdrawn, but will not be subject to the 10% early withdrawal penalty, imposed when amounts are withdrawn from an IRA before the taxpayer reaches the age of 59½.

QUALIFIED EXPENSES
The penalty-free IRA withdrawal is only available if the withdrawal is used to pay for qualified education expenses. Qualified education expenses include tuition, fees, books, supplies, and equipment. Room and board are also included if the student is enrolled on at least a half-time basis. These education expenses must be reduced by any tax-free scholarships or grants, qualified U.S. Series EE bonds, veterans' education benefits, and other tax-free educational benefits

ELIGIBLE STUDENTS
To be eligible for the penalty-free IRA distribution, the student must be the taxpayer, the taxpayer's spouse, or any child or grandchild of the taxpayer or the taxpayer's spouse at an eligible educational institution.

STUDENT LOAN INTEREST DEDUCTION

A tax deduction is allowed for interest paid on qualified student loans. The taxpayer does not have to itemize deductions to claim this deduction. The loans do not have to be federal interest-subsidized loans. Any type of loan that is used to pay college costs qualifies for this interest deduction. For example, a loan taken from your life insurance policy that is used to pay for college would qualify.

CALCULATION OF THE INTEREST DEDUCTION
The interest deduction is calculated by taking 100% of any interest due and paid on a qualified student loan.

MAXIMUM INTEREST DEDUCTION ALLOWED
The maximum interest deduction allowed is $2,500 per year.

INTEREST DEDUCTION PHASE-OUT
The deduction for student loan interest is phased-out when the taxpayer reaches certain

levels of modified AGI.

The AGI phase-out range for the student loan interest deduction is $50,000 to $65,000, for single taxpayers; and $100,000 to $130,000, for married taxpayers filing jointly.

> **Planning tip:** As a tax planning strategy, families where the families have modified AGI in excess of the phase-out levels and the student does not qualify for financial aid, may have the student take out Unsubsidized Federal Stafford Loans during college years. The student can take out these loans even though the student does not qualify for financial aid. The interest on these loans can be accrued and paid after the student leaves college. At that time, the student will be able to file a tax return and claim an exemption for the student and will probably be under the income phase-out levels. The student can then deduct the interest on the student's tax return.

QUALIFIED EXPENSES
The student loan interest deduction is only available for qualified expenses for undergraduate or graduate courses. The loan must have been used to pay the cost of attendance at an eligible educational institution. These expenses include tuition, fees, room and board, supplies, equipment, transportation and related personal expenses.

> **Note:** Qualified expenses for the interest deduction include more items than are allowed for the HC or LC.

Qualified expenses do not include expenses paid by an intra-family loan. Also, qualified expenses do not include expenses paid with a loan from a qualified employer retirement plan.

ELIGIBLE STUDENTS
To be eligible for the interest deduction, the student must be enrolled on at least a half-time basis, in a program leading to a degree, certificate, or other recognized educational credential. The student must be the taxpayer, the taxpayer's spouse, or a dependent of the taxpayer at the time the loans were received. No deduction is allowed for an individual who is claimed as a dependent on another taxpayer's tax return.

QUALIFIED EDUCATION LOAN
The loan must have been incurred solely to pay qualified higher education expenses at an eligible institution.

The higher education expenses must be paid or incurred within a reasonable period of time before or after the debt originates.

FINANCIAL AID CONSEQUENCES
The student loan interest deduction will increase the financial aid eligibility of any student who is currently enrolled in college. Since the interest deduction lowers the income of the parents or student, it could increase the financial aid eligibility by the amount of the interest deduction times the parents' financial aid income assessment rate of 22% to 47%, or the student's financial aid income assessment rate of 50%.

DEDUCTION FOR QUALIFIED HIGHER EDUCATION EXPENSES

An individual can claim a deduction for qualified tuition and related expenses paid during the year.

Eligible expenses for the deduction are qualified tuition and fees. Accordingly, tuition and fees for the taxpayer, the taxpayer's spouse, and a dependent qualify, including books, supplies, and equipment, if paid to the educational institution as a condition of enrollment or attendance. However, costs associated with room and board, student activities, transportation, and other expenses are not permitted.

HIGHER EDUCATION EXPENSE DEDUCTIONS

| Year | Modified AGI | | Maximum |
	Single	Joint	Deduction
2006	$0 - $65,000	$0 - $130,000	$4,000
2006	$65,001 - $80,000	$130,001 - $160,000	$2,000

No tuition deduction is permitted if the taxpayer elects to claim the Hope Scholarship or Lifetime Learning credit for the tax year.

Module 4
Tax Capacity

In this section we will explore how a family can save and pay for college in a tax-efficient manner.

INTRODUCTION TO TAX CAPACITY

When planning for college, you must be aware of the many income tax strategies available to increase the amount of family funds for future college costs. While these strategies may not produce a direct college benefit, like a grant or scholarship, they may produce tax benefits to your family as a whole, and therefore, increase the amount of family funds available to pay for college. To gain the maximum effect of these strategies, you must utilize the education tax incentives discussed in the prior section. The combination of the income tax strategies and education tax incentives described in this module will enable you to save and/or pay for college in a tax-efficient manner.

Because some families are not eligible for financial aid, they are not penalized by a loss of financial aid for shifting income and assets to their children.

Therefore, they should take full advantage of a child's lower tax bracket by shifting income and assets to the child. Accordingly, a key strategy is to focus on the benefits of the tax system. This will be driven by taking advantage of opportunities in the child's tax return (i.e., the child's lower tax bracket) not available to the parent or grandparent. Tax capacity is the amount of income that can be shifted to a child, and have the child still be taxed in a lower tax bracket than the parents' tax bracket.

TAX CAPACITY TIME FRAMES
A child's tax capacity can be divided into two time frames:

1.   Birth through age 17, the Kiddie Tax years

2.   Age 18 through College years

To properly plan the use of your child's tax return, you must understand your child's tax capacity and tax opportunities for each of these time frames.

Birth through Age 17 - Kiddie Tax Years
During the period from birth through age 17, a child's tax capacity is limited by the Kiddie Tax. The Kiddie Tax is applied to the investment income such as interest, dividends, or rental income, of a child under age 18 that exceeds $1,700. The investment income in excess of $1,700 is taxed at the parents' top tax rate, rather than the child's lower rate of 10% for ordinary income or 5% for capital gain. Earned income, such as wages, is not subject to the kiddie tax at any age.

The Kiddie Tax does not apply to the first $850 of investment income and, in addition, the child is allowed an $850 standard deduction. Therefore, a child's unearned income up to the greater of $1,700 or $850 plus itemized deductions will not be taxed at the parents' top tax rate.

> *Example: In 2006, a five-year old child has interest income of $900. Taxable income of $50 is subject to tax at the child's tax rate. Interest income of $900 less the standard deduction of $850 equals taxable income of $50. The Kiddie Tax does not apply because investment income does not exceed $1,700.*

Since the Kiddie Tax applies only to unearned income of a child under 18 years of age, one option for avoiding the Kiddie Tax is to invest the child's assets in investments that produce tax-exempt income or defers the income until after the child reaches age 18. Efficient use of the child's tax capacity, however, would suggest that the child can absorb at least $850 of unearned income, tax-free annually.

Age 18 and College Years

When a child reaches age 18, the Kiddie Tax rules no longer apply. Therefore, you should be aware of your child's increased tax capacity. This increased tax capacity should be factored into the college-funding plan.

> **Note:** A <u>dependent</u> child's standard deduction is limited to **the greater of**:
>
> 1. $850 **OR**
>
> 2. Earned income plus $300.
>
> *Example: In year 2006, a 17-year-old child has $3,000 in wages and $2,000 in unearned income. The child's standard deduction is $3,300.*

This amount of income can be shifted to the child from a parent or grandparent, and be sheltered from the parents' higher income tax bracket.

When a child enters college years, the tax capacity may be increased. If the child provides over half of his financial support, the child will be able to claim the personal exemption, which is $3,300 for year 2006. Therefore, the child's tax capacity for college years will be $39,100 for year 2006: $5,150 standard deduction + $30,650 lower rate bracket + $3,300 personal exemption. In addition, if the child has a tax liability, the tax liability can then be offset by the Hope or Lifetime Learning credit. These credits can only be claimed if the child is not a tax dependent of the parents. Note that the child does not have to provide over half of his financial support in order to claim these tax credits.

> *Example: Larry is a dependent on his parents' return during his high school years. Upon entering college, Larry claims himself as a dependent because he provides over one-half of his own support by paying tuition and room and board from his own funds. Assume that Larry has $4,500 in wages, $3,000 in interest and dividends, and a $9,000 IRA withdrawal.*
>
> *The following summarizes the tax treatment for his first college year:*

34

YEAR 2006	
Wages	$ 4,500
Interest/Dividends	3,000
IRA Withdrawal	9,000
Total	16,500
Less Personal Exemption	- 3,300
Less Standard Deduction	- 5,150
Taxable Income	$ 8,050
Tax	$ 830
Hope Credit	830
Total Tax	$ ---0---

Note: In order for a child to claim the personal exemption, the child must show that he is furnishing over half of his support. In determining whether the child furnished over half the support, the child's contribution to his support must be compared with the support received from all sources. The contribution includes money the child used for support, even if nontaxable, such as gifts, savings, Social Security, and other public assistance programs.

Support of a child includes the cost of food, clothing, the fair market value of shelter, medical and dental, child-care expenses, recreation, gifts and allowances, and education. The value of a scholarship or grant does not count in computing support, if the dependent is a child, stepchild, adopted child, or foster child, and the child is a full-time student.

Example: A child takes out $5,500 in loans and withdraws $8,000 from savings and uses the funds to pay for college. The child's parents only provided $6,000 toward the child's support during the year. The child can claim the personal exemption because the child provided over half of the support.

INCOME SHIFTING STRATEGIES

Income shifting from parents or grandparents, to children or grandchildren, to take advantage of the child's tax capacity is accomplished by putting income-producing assets in the children's or grandchildren's name. The related income generated by these assets is taxed at the child's lower income tax rates, and thus, the family receives a tax benefit. This tax benefit or "tax scholarship" will help increase the amount of funds available for college. In addition to the income tax savings, there may also be considerable estate tax savings earned by shifting the asset to a child or grandchild. Several income shifting techniques will be discussed in this section.

METHODS OF INCOME SHIFTING

Parents can shift assets and the resulting income, in one of many ways. Four of the most common ways to shift income are:

1. Gifting appreciated assets during college years

2. Compensating the child

3. Giving assets that will earn and grow

4. Gifts of business interest

Shifting by Gifting Appreciated Assets during College Years

Gifts of appreciated assets to the child from the parents may be an effective method of shifting income to the child. If the gift is not made until the child needs the money for college, the parent can keep control of the asset until it is needed for college.

> *Example: The parents normally had taxable income of $350,000. This income level made the parents ineligible to take a $3,300 tax exemption in 2006 for their child. The family's financial advisor suggested that they give $20,000 of stock each year through college years to the child. The annual stock gift had appreciated $15,000 since the parents bought it. In the following year when the child started college, the child would sell the stock and use it for college expenses. The tax consequences to the parents would be that they would not pay capital gains taxes of $2,250, 15% capital gains rate x $15,000 gain, on the $20,000 stock sale. Because the student could prove that the $20,000 was used for support and that it made up over half of annual support, the student could claim the $3,300 tax exemption on his tax return. The student would have taxable income of $11,700 ($15,000 gain - $3,300 exemption) and pay only $585 in income taxes (5% x $11,700). In addition, the student would be eligible to claim the Hope and Lifetime Learning credits that would reduce the student's tax liability to zero college years. Therefore, the total family tax savings would be $2,250 per year or $9,000 over the four years of college.*

Shifting Income by Compensating the Child

Parents with businesses or rentals that can pay compensation to the child will achieve tax benefits that can be used to pay for part of the college cost.

> *Example: A parent owns a sole-proprietorship business. The parent decides to hire his 15-year-old child to clean the business premises. The child was paid a reasonable wage of $4,000 per year and encouraged to save the earnings for future college costs. Since the parent was in a combined 41% tax bracket, federal 35% + state 6%, the $4,000 in wages paid to the child saved the parent $1,640 in taxes (41% x $4,000). Since the child's taxable income would be zero ($4,000 wages - $5,150 standard deduction), there would be no tax on the wages. Therefore, the total family tax savings would be $1,640 per year.*

In addition to the tax saving benefits of hiring a child, the child would be eligible to save for college, because of the earned income, by purchasing either Roth or regular IRAs. The tax-deferred growth over a long term can result in very substantial accumulations when the child reaches college age. The Roth IRA may be the best type of IRA to use because the original contributions may be withdrawn tax and penalty-free for college expenses. If the child has other unearned income that is creating income tax, a traditional IRA should be considered.

Shifting by Giving Assets that Earn and Grow in Pre-College Years
For parents with no appreciated assets or family compensation opportunities, an alternative strategy is to shift assets to the child as early as possible by annual gifts, so that the growth and earnings on the investments are taxed at the child's rates rather than parental rates.

In general, the strategy should be to defer all investment income to college years to take advantage of the education tax credits.

Use of a custodial account is a common vehicle to hold the assets shifted to a child in pre-college years. These accounts are simple and inexpensive to establish. The custodian of the account is responsible to see that the account assets are spent for the benefit of the child. This method of income-shifting could be utilized by parents who want to keep the control of the asset out of the child's hands until the child is 18 or 21 years of age. Parents can reduce their estate and provide a college fund for their child by using a custodial account. If the parents are giving a small or moderate amount of assets to their child and do not want the high administrative costs associated with trusts, a custodial account should be considered.

> **Planning tip:** Nonqualified stock options and incentive stock options, ISOs, can be used to shift income to children at capital gain rates. By making lifetime gifts of nonqualified stock options before the market value has appreciated, an employee may remove a potential high-growth asset from an estate, at a low gift tax value. By permitting an employee to transfer nonqualified stock options to children or grandchildren, a company may confer a substantial benefit without additional compensation expense and the employee will have an appreciated asset to gift to his children. The children will sell the stock to pay for college and will be taxed at the child's lower capital gain rates.

> **Planning tip:** If you are aware of an investment that has appreciation potential, instead of purchasing the investment, you could direct your child to make the investment. If necessary, sufficient cash or other assets can be given to your child so that he/she can make the purchase.

GIFTS OF BUSINESS INTEREST
There are other income-shifting techniques that may be employed by the parents to shift income to their child. The following techniques can be used to shift income to a child:

1. Gifts of S Corporation stock to the child to shift part of the earnings to the child

2. Gifts of Limited Liability Company interests to shift part of the earnings to the

child

3.   Gifts of Family Limited Partnership interests to shift part of the earnings to the child

INVESTMENTS FOR DEFERRING INCOME TO COLLEGE YEARS

There are several investments to defer income to college years to take advantage of a child's tax capacity. One or a combination of the following investments may be used to defer income to college years.

1.   Coverdell Education Savings Accounts

2.   Qualified Tuition Plans

3.   I Bonds and EE Bonds

4.   Traditional IRAs and SIMPLE IRAs

5.   Roth IRAs

6.   Tax-Efficient Funds

7.   Annuities

8.   Life Insurance

TAX CAPACITY COMPREHENSIVE EXAMPLE

Dr. Smith is a 45 year-old physician who earns $150,000 per year and has not saved for his 11 year-old son Johnny's college education. Dr. Smith is the sole shareholder and employee of an S-Corporation. The cost of Johnny's college education is estimated to be $150,000. Dr Smith's financial condition is as follows:

ASSETS:

Savings/ Investments	$ 40,000	
Residence	$400,000	
Rental Property	$100,000	
Medical Practice	$150,000	
Retirement	$150,000	
TOTAL ASSETS		$840,000

LIABILITIES

Credit Cards	$ 5,000	
Loans—Medical School	$ 40,000	
Home Mortgage	$200,000	
TOTAL LIABILITIES		$245,000

NET WORTH	$595,000

In this example, Dr. Smith wants to keep his savings and investments for emergency purposes and does not want to borrow from his retirement to send Johnny to college. The rental property of $100,000 provides a yearly income of $10,000 and is fully depreciated. Dr. Smith earns too much money to qualify for financial aid. To maximize his ability to save for Johnny's education, Dr. Smith takes the following financial steps when Johnny is 11 years old:

1. Dr. Smith takes out a second mortgage of $20,000 and purchases Treasury Bonds that will earn 7% interest.

2. Dr. Smith employs Johnny in his business at a salary of $3,000 per year, then $4,000 in his senior year of high school.

3. Dr. Smith will fund a Coverdell Education Savings Account for Johnny through his S-Corporation, in the amount of $2,000 per year. The corporation will receive a $2,000 deduction and Johnny will receive an additional $2,000 in income each year.

4. Dr. Smith and his wife will gift 25%, a value of $25,000, of their rental property each year for four years, beginning when Johnny turns 15 years old. This gift will allow Johnny to receive the full $10,000 of income, cash flow, from the rental property when he turns 18. Furthermore, Dr. Smith will have eliminated $100,000 from his estate.

5. Using the Tax Capacity model, Johnny will accumulate $110,051 in funds by the end of high school. The rental property will also provide an additional $10,000 in cash flow for each year of college, until he graduates. The final result will be

$150,051 in available funds for the estimated $150,000 cost of college. Furthermore, Dr. Smith will save $25,269 in taxes, which is the same as receiving $27,269 in scholarships.

Note: This model could have been initiated in earlier years to help pay for Johnny's private elementary and secondary school expenses.

The following **Exhibit 1** further illustrates the Tax Capacity example.

EXHIBIT 1

Year	2004	2005	2006	2007	2008	2009	2010	2011	Grand Total
Age of child	11	12	13	14	15	16	17	18	
Child's wages (1)	5,000	5,000	5,000	5,000	5,000	5,000	5,000	6,000	$ 41,000
Education IRA (contribution)									
Rental income (2)					2,500	5,000	7,500	10,000	25,000
Interest/dividends	1,400	1,400	1,400	1,400	1,400	1,400	1,400	1,400	11,200
Regular IRA deduction	(2,000)	(3,000)	(3,000)	(3,000)	(4,000)	(5,000)	(5,000)	(5,000)	(30,000)
Standard deduction	(5,150)	(5,150)	(5,150)	(5,150)	(5,150)	(5,150)	(5,150)	(5,150)	(41,200)
Personal exemption								(3,100)	(3,100)
Taxable income	(450)	(1,450)	(1,450)	(1,450)	(250)	1,250	3,750	4,450	9,450
Tax rate	10%	10%	10%	10%	10%	10/35%	10/35%	10%	
Tax liability before Hope Credit	-0-	-0-	-0-	-0-	-0-	438	1313	445	2,196
Hope Credit								(445)	(445)
Net tax liability	-0-	-0-	-0-	-0-	-0-	438	1313	-0-	1,751
Taxes parents would have paid (3)	2,240	2,240	2,240	2,240	3,115	3,990	4,865	6,000	27,020
Tax Savings	2,240	2,240	2,240	2,240	3,115	3,552	3,552	6,090	25,269
ACCUMULATED FUNDS (4)									
Rental Income, invested in 529 Plan with 7% earnings					2,675	8,212	16,812	28,689	28,689
Treasury bond fund (7%)	20,000	20,000	20,000	20,000	20,000	20,000	20,000	20,000	20,000
Corporate Education Savings Account	2,140	4,430	6,880	9,501	12,307	15,308	18,520	21,956	21,956
Child's regular IRA contribution	2,140	5,500	9,095	12,941	18,127	24,746	31,828	39,406	39,406
Total pre-college funds	24,280	29,930	35,975	42,442	53,109	68,266	87,160	110,051	110,051
Rental income—age 19									10,000
Rental income—age 20									10,000
Rental income—age 21									10,000
Rental income-age 22									10,000
TOTAL FUNDS AVAILABLE FOR COLLEGE									**$ 150,051**

(1) **Child's earnings include $2,000 per year from the corporate Coverdell Education Savings Account.**
(2) The husband and wife are each gifting $12,500 in rental property per year to the child.
(3) The parents' tax rate for this example is 35%.
(4) **All investments in this example grow at an annual rate of 7%.**

Module 5
Grandparents' and Relatives' Funds

In this section we will explore some strategies that can be employed by grandparents or relatives to help pay for educational costs.

Direct Gifts for Tuition

Gifts made directly to a college to pay for a student's tuition are considered a "resource" of the student and therefore reduce the financial need of the student on a dollar-for-dollar basis. Gifts given directly to a college, private elementary or high school for tuition do not reduce the donor's annual $12,000 gift tax exclusion. The gifts must be in cash.

> *Example: Grandpa consulted with his financial advisor, who was ignorant of the financial aid rules. He advised the grandparent to gift the $12,000 directly to the college for the tuition costs. When the grandchild received the financial aid award letter from the college, the grandchild noticed that the dollar amount of the award offer was reduced dollar-for-dollar by the $12,000 gift made directly to the college for tuition. This consequence could have been avoided if the financial advisor had understood the financial aid rules.*

The above strategy of gifting money directly to a college or to a K-12 private school for tuition may be a beneficial gifting strategy for families with children who will not be eligible for financial aid. Gifts for medical expenses paid directly to the medical provider also do not reduce the annual $12,000 gift exclusion.

Grandparents who wish to help pay for a grandchild's college education, who is eligible for financial aid, should avoid making gifts to the grandchild until after the grandchild is finished with college. The grandparent could gift the money to the grandchild after the grandchild finished college and the grandchild could then use the money to pay the student loans acquired during the college years. As an alternative, the grandparent could also loan the money to the grandchild during college years and then make the gift after college years. If the grandchild is not expected to qualify for financial aid, it is acceptable to make gifts to the grandchild or to make payments directly to the college.

> *Example: Grandma Lucy makes a cash gift of $12,000 to her granddaughter, Lil, during February 2006. Grandma Lucy also makes a payment of $17,200 for Lil's tuition directly to Minnesota University during 2007. Because the tuition was paid on behalf of Lil directly to the educational institution, the transfer is exempt from gift taxation. Additionally, because Grandma Lucy's other gifts to Lil during the year were $12,000 or less; no gift tax return is required to be filed by Grandma Lucy for the year 2007.*

QUALIFIED TUITION PLANS TO FUND A GRANDCHILD'S COLLEGE COST

If a grandparent wants to reduce the size of an estate and help pay for grandchildren's college educations, the grandparent should consider the use of Qualified Tuition Plans, QTPs, to accomplish these goals.

If the grandparent is young and in good health and anticipates living for quite awhile longer, the grandparent may want to make sure that there are adequate funds available for retirement needs. Also, the grandparent wants to insure that the grandchildren will not grow up to be spendthrifts and waste the money intended for college. Additionally, the grandparent may not like the idea of trusts or custodial accounts to accumulate funds for the grandchildren's college educations. If a grandparent uses these types of vehicles to accumulate funds, the grandparent will lose control of the money and it will not be available for retirement needs, and the grandchildren may not utilize it for college.

Because of the above concerns, funding grandchildren's college educations with a QTP may be the best option. The grandparent can establish an account for each grandchild and fund it with annual tax-free gifts, if the gift is less than the annual gift exclusion. The advantages of a QTP to fund a college education are:

1. The grandparent can withdraw the funds from the QTP if they should be needed for retirement.

2. The funds need not be distributed to a grandchild who might use the funds for non-college purposes.

3. If a grandchild falls from favor with the grandparent, the plan funds can be rolled over to another beneficiary.

4. The grandchildren will benefit from the deferral of income tax on the plan earnings.

   Example: Grandpa and Grandma have a combined estate of $3 million, which they wish to reduce. Additionally, they also want to help fund the college educations of their two grandchildren. They both plan to contribute $100,000 to the QTPs for each of their two grandchildren and establish QTPs for both of the children's parents. Each grandparent plans to contribute $100,000 to both of the individual QTPs for the parents. After these plans have been established, the grandparents switch the beneficiaries of these QTPs from the parents to the grandchildren. This switch does not trigger a tax or penalty since the grandchildren are qualified beneficiaries of the parents. However, in order for the parents to avoid a gift-tax liability, they must elect to spread the gift over five years on their gift tax return. The grandparents will reduce their estate by $800,000 through the use of QTPs and still keep control of the funds.

If a grandparent's primary goal is to reduce an estate in the most tax-efficient manner possible, a QTP may not be the best option. If the grandparent anticipates being alive during the grandchildren's college years, the best way to reduce a grandparent's estate may be for the grandparent to make gifts directly to the grandchildren's colleges. In this situation, the grandparent will not waste the annual gift exclusion on gifts to a QTP. If part or all of the annual gift exclusion is used to offset gifts to a QTP, the grandparent is not reducing the estate in the most tax-efficient manner. The grandparent could make gifts directly to colleges and also make additional gifts that could be offset by the annual gift exclusion.

> *Example: Grandma has a $5,000,000 estate and wants to reduce her estate in the most tax-efficient manner and pay for her two grandchildren's college educations. Both of the grandchildren will be attending a college where the annual tuition is $15,000 per year, and room and board is $10,000 per year. Grandma will pay the annual tuition payments for each of the grandchildren. This will reduce her estate by $120,000, $15,000 tuition per year x 4 years of college x 2 grandchildren. Grandma still has the $12,000 annual gift tax exclusion available to offset the gifts made to the grandchildren to pay for their annual room and board costs. Therefore, Grandma has transferred a total of $200,000 to the grandchildren without incurring any gift tax liability ($120,000 payments for tuition plus $80,000 in gifts to the grandchildren for payment of room and board).*

> *If Grandma gifts $200,000 in one year to individual QTPs for each grandchild and elects to spread the gifts over 5 years, Grandma would have a $20,000 per year gift to each grandchild over the 5-year period. Since these gifts would be over the annual $12,000 gift exclusion, Grandma would have taxable gifts of $8,000 per year per grandchild or a total of $80,000 in taxable gifts over the 5-year period.*

> *Alternatively, if Grandma was not certain that she would be alive during all of the college years of her two grandchildren, she could immediately gift the $80,000 that was to be used for room and board to individual QTPs for the two grandchildren, and wait until college years to make the $120,000 of gifts for tuition. If she elects to spread the $80,000 in gifts over a 5-year period, she will have no gift tax liability, $40,000 over 5 years will result in a gift of $8,000 per year, per grandchild.*

GRANDPARENT'S RETIREMENT ACCOUNTS TO FUND COLLEGE

Grandparents that are under age 59½ may withdraw funds from a traditional or Roth IRA to pay for a grandchild's qualified college expenses without incurring the 10% early withdrawal penalty. Paying for a grandchild's college education by withdrawing funds from an IRA will reduce the value of the IRA in a grandparent's estate. Since IRAs are considered "income-in-respect-of-decedent," IRD, assets in a grandparent's estate and receive adverse tax treatment, it may be best for the grandparent to use IRAs, rather than non-IRD assets to pay for a grandchild's college education.

As an alternative to naming a grandchild as the beneficiary of an IRA, a grandparent, who had charitable intentions, could make a charity the beneficiary of an IRA. The IRA would then not be eaten up by taxes. The grandparent could buy life insurance for the grandchild to replace the IRA value. The policy should be put in an irrevocable life insurance trust to keep it out of the grandparent's estate. If the trust document permitted it, the grandchild could borrow from the cash value of the life insurance to fund college.

CHARITABLE GIFTING

In order for charitable gifting to be a viable college funding strategy, you must have a charitable desire. The donor will not receive more tax or college benefits from a donation than the monetary cost of the donation. The effective tax rate would have to be 100% in order for the donor to receive full tax value for the donation. Therefore, the donor must have a desire to give to a charitable cause for reasons other than monetary gain.

It may make sense for the donor who has a charitable desire to combine the estate and tax benefits of a charitable donation with a desire to help pay for a grandchild's college education. One strategy would be to use a charitable trust to accomplish the grandparent's goals of reducing income and estate taxes, gifting to a charity, and funding a grandchild's college education. This could be accomplished through the use of a Charitable Remainder Trust, CRT. These trusts can be created during the donor's lifetime or at death.

The advantages of establishing a CRT would be:

1.   The parents receive a current tax deduction.

2.   The donated asset is not included in the donor's estate.

3.   Future income generated by the asset is not subject to income tax.

4.   The asset's appreciation is not subject to estate tax.

The disadvantages of establishing the CRT would be:

1.   The donor loses the lifetime financial benefits generated by the donated asset.

2.   The donor's heirs will have a reduced inheritance.

Example: The grandparents have stock worth $50,000 with a tax basis of $5,000. The grandparents contributed the stock to a 4-year term CRT and gifted the annual income interest of $6,000, based on a 12% return, to their grandchild.   The income interest proceeds were to be used for the grandchild's college expenses.

The income interest of $6,000 is taxable to the grandchild. In addition, the grandparents have made a gift, of approximately $20,000, to the grandchild of the present interest in the CRT income interest. At the end of the trust, *the named charity would receive the trust principal. In addition to avoiding paying taxes on the appreciation of $45,000 ($50,000 - $5,000), the grandparents will receive approximately a $30,000 charitable income tax deduction.*

Planning Tip: A CRT is exempt from income tax. Therefore contributing a highly appreciated, low-yielding asset to the CRT, can often increase a donor's cash flow. The asset can then be sold and the proceeds reinvested in a higher-yielding investment without depleting the investment principal. This can increase a donor's cash flow from low-yielding assets.

TESTAMENTARY TRUST FOR FUNDING COLLEGE

A grandparent can provide funds for a grandchild's college education through a will with a Testamentary Trust.

A provision in the Testamentary Trust could be made for general living expenses, as defined as typical support, maintenance, education and health expenses, until the grandchild reaches the age of 18. Once the grandchild reaches the age of 18, the general living expenses of the grandchild would be included as a portion of the grandchild's educational and health expenses. If the grandchild wished to have his living expenses to continue being paid by the trust, the grandchild would have to be satisfactorily engaged in the pursuit of a college education. In essence, the grandparent would be "ruling from the grave."

A Testamentary Trust could benefit one, two, or more grandchildren. To prevent an older grandchild from pillaging the fund down at the expense of a younger grandchild, "equalization provisions" in the trust should be considered. In the alternative, the trust document should contain provisions mandating or allowing the breaking of the original trust for the benefit of two or more grandchildren into separate trusts for the benefit of each separate grandchild.

GRANDPARENTS USE OF TAX CAPACITY

A grandparent should consider incorporating the same strategies that parents use to maximize the grandchild's tax capacity. These strategies allow a grandparent to lower income, gift, and estate taxes.

Module 6
Controlling The Cost Of College

You should be aware of certain cost cutting strategies and academic strategies to cut the actual cost of attending college. If these strategies can be implemented, they will diminish the burden of paying for college just as much as winning a scholarship for your child.

Cost Cutting Strategies

Combination Undergraduate-Graduate Degree
If the student is certain to head for graduate school after college, the student may want to consider a college that allows a student to pursue a Master's degree or Doctorate while completing a B.A. degree in three years. There are approximately 350 colleges (the book *College Board Index of Majors and Graduate Degrees* lists these colleges) that have this type of program. These programs usually require students to take extra courses during the college year and summers.

If the student completes a Bachelor's degree in three years instead of four, the student can save a year of college costs. In addition, the student will be able to start a career a year earlier.

> *Example: If the student could save a year of college costs, at $25,000 per year, and earn an extra year of pay at a job of $25,000, the individual will be ahead by $50,000 and cut 50% from the cost of college.*

Guaranteed Tuition
A few colleges guarantee their tuition for four years at the time of enrollment, at no obligation to the student to attend for the entire four years. Under other plans, families can prepay tuition for the entire four years in one lump sum and escape subsequent tuition increases. If a family borrows a home equity loan to pay this lump sum, the home interest expense could reduce the income tax liability.

Taking advantage of such programs could reduce the family's overall college expenses. However, the family may want to consider whether a return on investment can be achieved that is equivalent to or better than the rate of tuition increases, while still having the use of the money.

The financial aid office should be consulted before purchasing one of these plans to determine if the plan locks the student into attending that particular college and what happens to the money paid into the program in the event the student does not attend the college or does not complete the entire 4 years.

The family should also be aware that if the student happens to qualify for need-based financial aid, these programs are treated as a student "resource" and reduce a student's financial aid on a dollar-for-dollar basis.

Transfer From a Low-cost Public to a Prestigious Private
Some students may attend a low-cost public university (or junior college) for one or two

years, and then transfer to a prestigious, and more expensive, private college. The tuition cost savings can be substantial for the family and the student will get a degree from the prestigious college.

Establish In-State Residency
If the student can establish in-state residency, the cost of college can be reduced by eliminating the out-of-state tuition. In many states, out-of-state tuition can almost double the cost of attendance.

The four basic elements used to determine residency are:

1.   Duration requirement

2.   Financial independence

3.   Proof of residency

4.   Non-academic purpose

> **Note:** The student cannot be listed as a dependent on the parents' tax return.

Duration Requirement
The standard duration residency requirement is usually 12 months. The student is required to maintain a "continuous presence" in the state for a period of 12 months. Unless the student takes a full year off from college, in-state status normally will begin with the second (sophomore) year. The student must complete this mandatory requirement prior to obtaining the benefits of in-state tuition. This rule is used to determine students' true fixed intention regarding their permanent place of residency.

Financial Independence
Financial independence is another mandatory requirement. Again, it is important to correspond with school officials to determine the specific rules regarding financial independence at a specific school. They will look at a student's specific employment situation in order to determine whether or not the student is truly independent of the parents or legal guardian.

Financial independence requires that a student cannot receive more than 50 percent of the income from an out-of-state source. Students must show that they can support themselves, make their own decisions and establish residency all on their own. Schools will look for "state sources of income" from employment of at least 50%. If the student is receiving significant support and income from a source outside of the state, the school will view this as a reason to support a denial for residency.

Proof of Residency
Establishing state residency is a matter of providing evidence as proof. The eight major elements used to determine residency are:

1.   Ownership of residence

2.   Full-time employment

3.   Type of employment

4.   Professional licensing

5.   State sources of income

6.   Payment of state income tax

7.   Personal property owned within state

8.   Aid received from other states

Ownership of a home or residence provides strong proof of residency, especially in a state where a student already has relatives and friends. Home ownership is an important factor in these states, which make it difficult for students to achieve in-state residency. However, most schools do not require home ownership, but consider it a major benefit if the student does own a home. In these cases, the student should at least establish a year-round lease or rental agreement.

Full-time employment is one of the best ways to establish residency and take away the school's subjective discretion. Full-time employment for 12 months is something the student should undertake to ensure in-state residency and tuition reclassification.

Ideally, the students should enter the field or type of employment that follows their basic course of study at the school, or is viewed as career employment. Part-time employment, in a job normally associated with students, allows the school the argument that the student is in the state only to receive an education.

Colleges and universities put great emphasis upon obtaining a professional license (real estate, insurance, brokers, etc.) from their specific state, and individuals obtaining such a professional license have a much stronger case to argue residency.

The student's source of income is an important factor and is frequently used by schools to deny residency. Be sure to check the state's requirements regarding "sources of income", as this may be a strategic requirement. If a gift is made to the student and the amount is sufficiently large, a school may interpret this gift as an attempt on the parent's part to support the student and thereby deny residency.

Students should file the respective state's income tax return, including state tax paid on any out-of-state income. Many schools place great emphasis on this requirement and view this as a strategic choice of state for residency.

Proof that the student has moved all personal belongings makes a strong case for in-state residency. A receipt slip from a public storage facility should provide significant evidence of this factor.

Students must make every effort to obtain all support and income from the state in which they seek residency. Parents should not be co-borrowers on student loans; however, in most cases, they can be a guarantor of the loan.

Non-academic Reasons for Coming to the State
Students should show non-academic reasons for their presence in a state. The best way to accomplish this is full-time employment and part-time course load while establishing the 12-month duration requirement. Students should also emphasize their non-educational activities, such as full-time or part-time business, local Chamber of Commerce membership of and even playing on the local softball team.

To obtain more detailed information on how to establish in-state residency, you should purchase the book, "How To Cut Tuition" by Daryl F. Todd.

Academic Strategies

Advanced Placement (AP) Studies
Perhaps the easiest and most effective way for a student to stand out academically for admissions is to score well on Advanced Placement tests offered by the College Board (www.collegeboard.com). While these studies are for the academically gifted student, they can represent real dollar reductions in the cost of college. The student can receive a full year's credit and be granted sophomore standing from more than 1,400 higher education institutions by earning satisfactory grades on enough AP Examinations.

Advanced Placement is awarded by the college or university, not by the College Board. Some institutions specify certain courses or other requirements for sophomore standing. The college's catalog usually provides a detailed description of that institution's Advanced Placement policy. Credit is usually awarded when one is admitted, although some colleges and universities award sophomore standing only after the student has demonstrated the ability to do satisfactory college work.

> **Planning tip:** When AP courses are added to the student's curriculum, the result is a "weighted grade point average" (WGPA), such as 4.3 on a 4.0 scale. This may help with admissions, but check with the institution the student is interested in attending to get a complete description of its AP policy before assuming that the student will get an AP credit.

AP exams are offered in a variety of subjects and are scored on a scale of 1 to 5, with 5 being the highest. The College Board gives these tests each May. Many high schools offer students practice tests to familiarize themselves with the format.

Some of the numerous benefits of AP courses are:

1.   Study a subject in greater depth

2.   Prepare for college caliber work

3.   Improve the chances of getting into a competitive college

4.   Increase the grade point average (GPA)

5.   Reduce college costs

6.   Increase time for special interest courses at college

7. Increase the options for double majors or upper level courses

8. Improve the ability to succeed in college

9. Increase eligibility for an AP Scholar Award (discussed in next section)

Internship/Co-op Education Programs
Internships for research and advanced studies are available at some colleges for the undergraduate student. Most are available to college juniors and seniors with outstanding academic records. These programs are usually funded by endowments contributed by alumni benefactors for specific fields of study. Options vary from working during the academic year or during summers, while some require the student to take time off from classes for specific research. Some colleges have applications for these internships, which are judged and decided upon objectively by a panel or committee. Other colleges have subjective, direct placement programs for internships.

> **Note:** Vault.com offers an on-line source of career and internship information. The website lists information on a wide range of internships and also includes hyperlinks to more than 3,000 corporate message boards, so that students can check out the pros and cons of any company's programs with employees and former interns before signing on.

Co-op education programs are formalized arrangements between the college and specific firms and corporations that allow the student to alternate full-time enrollment with full-time employment. Students usually alternate semesters in jobs directly related to their field of study. In addition to helping students finance part of their studies, it allows them to develop concrete job skills and experience that will enhance their employability after graduation.

> **Planning tip:** Co-op programs have become more popular lately, especially in technical programs such as accounting and computer science. These programs give the company an opportunity to review the student's attitude and work ethic and many hire the student prior to graduation. Co-op programs not only reduce the student's cost of college, but also offer immediate job placement. In a competitive job field, these programs can reduce the intangible costs associated with the time and effort of job hunting.

College Level Examination Programs (CLEP)
CLEP is the most widely accepted credit-by-examination program in the United States today. While Advanced Placement (AP) courses are usually taken by above average students, CLEP exams seem to benefit the average student and also the non-traditional (Adult Ed) student. More than 2,800 colleges and universities now award credit for satisfactory scores on CLEP exams.

The CLEP program can help students:

1. Save time

2. Save money

3.   Advance to more specialized courses

CLEP exams give students the opportunity to demonstrate college-level knowledge they have gained through prior study, independent study, professional experience, and cultural pursuits. In return, the student receives course credit, course exemption, or Advanced Placement toward a degree.

CLEP exams can save students time and money and put them on a faster track towards a college degree. High scores on CLEP exams can earn students as much as two years' college credit!

Frequently Asked Questions about the CLEP Program
Who is eligible to take CLEP exams?
Anyone can take one or more of the 34 CLEP exams available. Students should take the exams for which they feel they are best prepared. Students enrolled in college should first check the college's CLEP policy before taking any exam. Any student not yet enrolled should first check the list of Colleges Granting CLEP Credit.

How can I register for a CLEP Exam?
Contact your college test center, a local test center or even the national test center closest to you about their CLEP registration procedures and schedule. Each institution has its own procedures for student registration.

How much does it cost to take a CLEP Exam?
The test is approximately $46 plus the test center administration fee (generally $10).

How many CLEP exams may the student take?
Students are not limited to the number of exams they may take; however, most colleges and universities specify the maximum number of credits that can be granted. Check with your college for their policy.

Does my CLEP score count in my grade-point average?
Generally, a student is given credit by the college or university but no letter grade.

For which courses can I get credit?
This is determined by each college's credit-by-examination and CLEP policy.

Can CLEP credits be transferred?
Yes. Check the CLEP policy of the institution to which a student wishes to transfer.

How do I prepare for a CLEP exam?
Use The Official Study Guide for the CLEP Examinations published by College Board, talk with advisers and faculty, and review textbooks in the appropriate subject area and other relevant sources.

Similar to Advanced Placement (AP) and SAT examinations, CLEP exams are conducted by the College Board (Educational Testing Systems). Their website is www.collegeboard.com.

Distance Learning
Distance Learning (DL), also known as Distance Education (DE), is simply learning from a distance, usually from home, or from a conveniently located off-campus site. DL allows adults to earn college credits, even entire degrees, without ever leaving home. DL makes use of the Internet, software, modems, TV stations, 2-way television using fiber optics, microwave, and digital phone lines, satellites, radio, ham radio, videocassette and audio tape, and the ever-popular mailbox, to deliver instruction.

Anyone who needs flexibility or just wants to reduce costs may find distance learning to be the best way to combine studies and life. The reduction in education costs can be considerable, from room costs to transportation to savings in time.

However, distance learning does require well-motivated, self-disciplined students who are able to manage their time and set deadlines. It's easy for distance learners to neglect coursework because of personal or professional circumstances--unless they have compelling reasons to stay on track.

DL is for people who want to learn a new skill, or just pick up a few new ideas for the fun of learning. It is also a growing part of public and private schools from elementary level through high school, in many areas such as math, science, and languages.

Home schooling is also a type of DL. Typically, a home-schooled child is taught by the parents. Occasionally, the child is tutored at home in part or completely via modem or TV course.

DL is part of all degree types, from the A.A. to the Ph.D., and is an option in most majors, and at hundreds of universities worldwide. DL also includes non-credit courses, workshops, seminars and career credits like continuing education credits. Even though DL degrees do not follow a traditional course of study in classrooms, they are awarded based on the DL equivalent of college credits earned.

For most students, DL remains primarily a book and paper proposition, as well as an independent study effort, but is made more convenient with the delivery of information via the Internet, the web, online services, telephone, TV, satellite courses, VHS tapes, cassette tapes, records, radio, ham radio, and CD-ROM.

Many DL programs are correspondence courses where books, materials, and coursework are exchanged through the mail. However, there are courses that are completely electronic, such as interactive multimedia courses, and group learning in virtual classrooms.

DL also involves testing out of courses (CLEP exams) by demonstrating subject mastery through a single examination and earning college credit for life and work experience. Many people complete long unfinished Bachelor's degrees through the use of these CLEP exams.

Cutting the Time in College

Very few students graduate from college in four years. Most take five or more years to graduate. The reasons for the extra time needed to graduate are improper college selection and career assessment. Every time a student switches colleges or changes majors this usually means another year in college. To keep the time in college to four years the student must spend enough time and effort in college selection and career assessment. Following are checklists that can help the student in these areas:

Calendar of Events

There are many financial and academic deadlines that a family must be aware of to insure that no financial or academic opportunities are missed. Missing one of these deadlines may cost the family money or cost the student admission to a particular college or scholarships at the college. Every family should have a calendar of events to insure meeting important deadlines.

CHAPTER 2
PARENTS' MONEY FOR COLLEGE AND RETIREMENT

Module 1
Cash Flow for College and Retirement

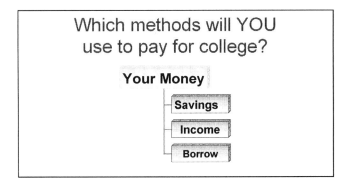

Do you have a game plan laid out for funding college? It could cost you a lot of hard-earned money if you don't.

After using Other People's Funds, which methods will YOU use to pay for college?

If you use your money, will you draw from savings accounts, pay for it out of your current income, or borrow the money?

CASH FLOW FOR COLLEGE AND RETIREMENT

If you want to invest funds from your current income to save for education and retirement costs, you must first determine if your cash flow can be increased to free up funds to save.

Ideally, you should save an amount that will not interfere with your current lifestyle.

To increase your cash flow you can decrease discretionary expense items, such as entertainment or travel.

Alternatively, you can increase your current cash flow by consolidating short-term debt into long-term debt. Debt consolidation will allow you to make smaller monthly payments.

In addition, there may be tax benefits achieved through debt consolidation, such as a home mortgage interest deduction.

CASH MANAGEMENT STRATEGIES

Some strategies that can increase your cash flow follow.

1. Minimize nonessential current discretionary expenditures.

2. A part-time, full-time, or temporary job might be considered to reach a specific savings goal.

3. You might consider delaying retirement plans. Working for a longer period can make a significant difference in your retirement picture. For example, in addition to continued earnings, working longer may provide continued fringe benefits and continued contributions to retirement plans.

4. You should maintain a cash reserve to meet emergency needs. Building an adequate reserve can help you avoid having to liquidate other investments when the market is depressed or it is otherwise inadvisable to sell.

5. You should consider allocating a lesser amount of funds to other parts of the financial plan. For example, education costs for children or grandchildren may need to be revised.

6. Debt should be minimized as you approach retirement. If borrowing is necessary, home equity loans or borrowing from a qualified retirement plan, if permitted, should be considered.

7. A reverse mortgage is a loan in the form of monthly payments or a lump sum payment against the equity in your personal residence. You may consider a reverse mortgage for many reasons, including one or more of the following:

    A. paying off personal debts
    B. paying for medical care
    C. covering financial emergencies
    D. supplementing monthly income

8. Use tax-deferred arrangements to maximize retirement income.

9. Your financial planner can incorporate investment planning into your retirement planning to make asset allocation recommendations that will enable you to meet retirement goals.

10. After gaining an understanding of your investment risk profile and reviewing your current investment portfolio, your financial planner might recommend that you be more aggressive in selecting among investment alternatives to enhance the possibility of a higher total return.

11. Retirement plans or accounts that allow you and/or your employer to make tax-deductible contributions to defer tax on the earnings within the plan or account are effective vehicles for retirement saving. Generally, it is best for you to invest long-term investment dollars in these tax-deferred vehicles before making long-term investments outside of such accounts.

MONTHLY CONTRIBUTION WORKSHEET

Following is a sample of a monthly contribution worksheet that you can use to manage and increase your cash flow:

Monthly Contribution Worksheet
John and Mary Jones

INFLOWS

Salary:		
Husband's Salary	2900	
Wife's Salary	100	
Total Salary		3000
Self-employed Income:		
Husband	100	
Wife	100	
Total Self-employed Income		200
Interest Income		
Checking	100	
Savings	100	
Other Interest	100	
Total Interest Income		300
Other Income		300
Gifts Received		100
Federal Tax Refund		100
State Tax Refund		100

TOTAL INFLOWS   4,100

OUTFLOWS

Mandatory Expenses

Advertising		
Auto		100
Fuel	100	
Insurance	100	
Registration	100	
Service	100	
Total Auto		400
Bank Charges		100
Charity		100
Clothing		100
Dining		100
Dues & Memberships		100
Gifts Given		100
Groceries		100
Household		100
Insurance:		
Home	100	
Life Insurance – Husband	100	
Life Insurance – Wife	100	
Total Insurance		300
Interest Expense:		
Mortgage	100	
Other	100	
Total Interest Expense		200
Medical Expense		
Doctor	100	
Health Insurance	100	
Medical Reimbursement	100	
Medicine	100	

Other	100	
Total Medical Expense		500
Mandatory expenses		**2300**
Discretionary Expenses		
Office Expense		100
Personal Expense		100
Postage		100
Professional Fees		100
Subscriptions		100
Taxes:		
Federal	100	
Medicare	100	
Property	100	
Social Security	100	
State	100	
Total Taxes		500
Utilities:		
Cable TV		
Fuel		
Gas & Electric		
Telephone		
Water		
Total Utilities		800
Total Discretionary expenses		**1800**
TOTAL OUTFLOWS		**4,100**
NET (INFLOWS - OUTFLOWS)	$	**-- 0 --**

DEBT CONSOLIDATION

Families can significantly increase their cash flow by debt consolidation. By consolidating their debt payments into one lower cost payment, families can increase cash flow to pay college expenses, fund their retirement and even pay off their home mortgage earlier than anticipated once the student is out of college.

The theory behind debt consolidation is simple. Home equity is one of the family's main assets, yet home equity is a very unproductive asset. You can only increase home equity by one of two ways: increase the value of your home, or decrease the debt owed on it. Otherwise, the home equity asset remains dormant and unproductive until you sell your home. The only way to make home equity productive, during the time you own the home, is to borrow the excess equity and wisely use the increased cash flow for productive purposes; such as paying off your high interest installment loans or credit cards.

By refinancing the family's personal residence, the old mortgage and all other high-interest, high-cost debt can be paid off with a new, lower-cost mortgage. The result is a lower monthly payment that creates extra cash flow that can be used to pay college expenses. There may also be additional tax deductions available with the new mortgage that can further increase your cash flow availability.

Example: The Smith family would like to send their children, Johnny, a high school senior, and Sally, a high school sophomore, to college. Mr. and Mrs. Smith earn a total of $75,000 per year in income, but have saved absolutely no *money to cover Johnny and Sally's educational expenses. Johnny and Sally plan to contribute to their own education by taking out student loans, but the Smiths will still need around $80,000 to fund the balance of both educations. The Smiths have few assets and considerable debt, and estimate that they can only contribute $400 per month, $4,800 per year, from their current income towards educational expenses, without dramatically changing their present lifestyle. The Smiths decide to refinance their current $120,000 in debt, mortgage and high cost consumer debt, into a new 30-year mortgage for $134,400.*

	Before consolidation		*After consolidation*	
	Monthly payment	*Balance*	*Monthly payment*	*Balance*
Mortgage	*$ 665*	*$ 84,500*	*$894*	*$134,400*
Car loans	*$ 420*	*$ 22,500*		
Credit cards	*$ 220*	*$ 7,800*		
Furniture	*$ 150*	*$ 5,200*		
Total	*$1,455*	*$120,000*	*$894*	*$134,400*

Using the debt consolidation example, the Smiths will achieve a considerably lower monthly payment, $894 versus $1,455, and increase their cash flow by $561 per month. They will also receive a lump sum cash amount of $14,400 from the new mortgage. This additional cash flow, combined with the student loans and the Smiths' $400 per month contribution from current income, will allow the Smiths to accomplish all three goals:

1. Fund Johnny and Sally's education expenses

2. Pay off their new 30-year mortgage in 13 years

3. Accumulate an additional $227,723 for retirement

The Smiths will not have to change their current financial lifestyle or tap into their retirement funds in an effort to pay for their children's college educations.

The Cash Flow Analysis Table that follows demonstrates the Smith's personal residence loan strategy. This model can also be used to fund Johnny and Sally's private elementary and secondary school expenses.

CASH FLOW ANALYSIS FOR DEBT CONSOLIDATION

Year	Annual Parental Contribution	Annual Student Contribution	Annual Mortgage Payment	Annual College Payment	Net Cash Flow	Year-end Retirement Account Balance	Year-end Mortgage Loan Balance	Estimated Year-end Home value	Age of Older Parent
						7.00%	7.00%	2.50%	
0	$14,400	$0	$0	$0	$14,400	$14,400	$134,400	$168,000	
1	$22,260	$0	$10,730	$9,975	$1,555	$17,072	$133,035	$172,200	48
2	$22,260	$0	$10,730	$9,730	$1,800	$20,193	$131,571	$176,505	49
3	$22,260	$0	$10,730	$19,658	($8,128)	$12,909	$130,001	$180,918	50
4	$22,260	$0	$10,730	$20,172	($8,642)	$4,566	$128,318	$185,441	51
5	$22,260	$0	$10,730	$9,815	$1,715	$6,720	$126,513	$190,077	52
6	$22,260	$0	$10,730	$10,581	$949	$8,206	$124,577	$194,828	53
7	$22,260	$0	$10,730	$0	$11,530	$21,117	$122,502	$199,699	54
8	$22,260	$0	$10,730	$0	$11,530	$34,933	$120,277	$204,692	55
9	$22,260	$0	$10,730	$0	$11,530	$49,715	$117,891	$209,809	56
10	$22,260	$0	$10,730	$0	$11,530	$65,532	$115,332	$215,054	57
11	$22,260	$0	$10,730	$0	$11,530	$82,457	$112,588	$220,431	58
12	$22,260	$0	$10,730	$0	$11,530	$100,566	$109,646	$225,941	59
13	$22,260	$0	$10,730	$0	$11,530	$119,942	$106,491	$231,590	60
14	$22,260	$0	$0	$0	$22,260	$38,211	$0	$237,380	61
15	$22,260	$0	$0	$0	$22,2606	$64,704	$0	$243,314	62
16	$22,260	$0	$0	$0	$22,260	$93,051	$0	$249,397	63
17	$22,260	$0	$0	$0	$22,260	$123,383	$0	$255,632	64
18	$22,260	$0	$0	$0	$22,260	$155,838	$0	$262,023	65
19	$22,260	$0	$0	$0	$22,260	$190,565	$0	$268,573	66
20	$22,260	$0	$0	$0	$22,260	$227,723	$0	$275,288	67
Totals	$459,600	$0	$139,490	$79,932	$240,178	$227,723	$0	$275,288	67

Module 2
Parents' Loans for College

In this section we will explore various loan options for parents.

PARENTS' LOANS FOR COLLEGE

For parents who do not have funds currently available for college because their funds are tied up in their business, in high-yielding investments, in retirement accounts, or in their residence, borrowing the funds for college may be a viable college-funding alternative.

FEDERAL PLUS LOANS

Federal PLUS, Parents' Loans for Undergraduate Students, Loans are not need-based loans. The borrower pays the interest and repayment begins immediately. However, if the parent is enrolled in college on at least a half-time basis, the repayment may be deferred while the parent is in college.

The interest rate on Federal PLUS Loans is variable with an upper limit of 9%. If a parent is not creditworthy and cannot obtain a PLUS Loan, the student can borrow an additional $4,000 per year in Unsubsidized Stafford Loans for the first and second years of college and $5,000 for the third, fourth, and fifth years of college. The amount of a PLUS Loan that a parent can borrow is limited to the COA, cost of attendance, minus the financial aid award offered to the student.

Graduate and Professional students are now eligible to take PLUS Loans in their names. Like parents under current law, these students will now be authorized to borrow up to the cost of attendance minus other aid received.

These are signature loans in the parent's name. If the signatory parent dies or becomes disabled before the loan is repaid, the remaining loan principal balance is forgiven. Only one parent must sign for the loan. PLUS Loans may be consolidated into one loan and repaid over a period of up to 30 years.

> *Example: If the COA at a college is $25,000 and the amount of financial aid offered was $12,000, the parents would be eligible for a $13,000 PLUS Loan. If the financial aid offer of $12,000 contained a $2,000 college work-study award and the student declined the work-study portion of the aid offered, the parents would then be eligible for a $15,000 PLUS Loan. However, if the student was offered no financial aid because the student demonstrated no financial need, the parents would be eligible for a $25,000 PLUS Loan.*

> **Observation:** If a student will be attending a college that assesses home equity, a home equity loan may be preferable to a Federal PLUS Loan. The home equity loan will reduce the value of the home. In addition, the interest on the home equity loan is not limited to $2,500 or by the parents' AGI.

Should a student be attending a college that will assess the personal residence equity, parents should consider taking an equity loan on the personal residence, rather than taking out the Federal PLUS Loan. The home equity loan will reduce the value of the personal residence and therefore, increase the student's financial aid eligibility by the amount of the decrease in residence equity, times the parental asset assessment rate of 5.6%.

Example: A home equity loan of $12,000 will lower the value of the personal residence by that amount. Since the assessment rate for parents' assets is 5.6%, the student would be eligible for an increase in financial aid of $672 per year, $12,000 x 5.6%, annually.

PERSONAL RESIDENCE LOANS

A personal residence loan may be a viable source of funds for college. Although many parents do not want to mortgage their home to pay for college costs, it may be a better source of funds than borrowing on their business assets or from their retirement accounts.

If you use a home equity line of credit to fund college, you will borrow what is needed, as it is needed, and therefore, you will pay interest only on the amount borrowed. You are usually allowed to make minimum monthly payments and you can make larger payments after your child is done with college. Since the interest rate is variable, the monthly payments will vary. There may be high loan fees associated with this type of loan.

If you use a second mortgage to fund college, you will borrow a fixed amount. Generally, there is a fixed interest rate and a fixed repayment schedule. Therefore, you will have a fixed monthly payment amount. Since you will be borrowing a lump sum, which probably will not be used all at once, you will be paying interest on money not currently needed. Therefore, you should consider investing the excess funds in a short-term investment until the funds are needed.

For parents whose income is too high to take advantage of the student loan interest deduction, a personal residence loan can give them an itemized income tax deduction, subject to the phase-out rules for high income. This deduction is not limited to $2,500, as is the case for student loan interest.

The repayment term on residence loans is usually longer than retirement account loans and other types of loans, which makes the monthly payments smaller.

Planning tip: For the conservative long-term investors, aggressively prepaying a home mortgage to avoid high interest costs can pay big dividends as a college and retirement strategy. The longer you stay in a home, the larger the cash flow savings.

Example: Joe has 15 years to go before his son attends college. Joe has a 30-year, $200,000 mortgage at an 8% rate. If Joe pays an extra $500 per month towards his loan, he'll pay off the mortgage in 14 years and save $193,000 in interest, an increase in cash flow. Plus, Joe will have created a minimum of $200,000 in equity (line of credit) to borrow against when his son goes to college.

If he pays an extra $200 per month, he will pay off his mortgage in 20 years *and save $125,000 in interest costs. Regardless of the amount of prepayment, once the mortgage is paid off, the amount no longer needed for monthly mortgage payments, can be used to pay college costs or invest for retirement.*

Caution: Prepaying a home mortgage reduces a source of low-cost financing and the ability to use tax-favored mortgage financing for college. Mortgage interest is tax-deductible only on borrowing used to acquire a home and up to $100,000 on subsequent financing. Prepaying will reduce the value for tax-deductible borrowing.

Example: Your home is worth $300,000 and the mortgage is paid down to $200,000 through normal payments. A home-equity loan of $100,000 can be used to borrow against the home's full value. If prepayments of $50,000 have also been made, reducing the mortgage balance to $150,000, you can only borrow against $250,000 of your home's value with deductible interest--$50,000 of its value will not qualify for deductible borrowing.

Planning tip: When trying to determine whether to use money to prepay your mortgage or as investment consider the following when making your decision: What is your time horizon? What is the interest rate on your mortgage? What is your income tax rate? You can calculate your after-tax mortgage cost by taking: [your mortgage rate x (1 – your tax rate)]. You can compare this to the after-tax returns you expect from the market over a period of time. The mortgage cost is fixed, but the market returns do carry risk. However, this can help you make an informed decision.

MARGIN ACCOUNT LOANS

If you have most assets tied up in stocks, bonds and mutual funds, you may want to borrow against the investment account rather than sell part of the investment to pay for college. You continue to receive dividends on the entire account and do not have to pay current income tax on the appreciation of the asset. The loan and accrued interest must be repaid before the stock is sold and the proceeds issued to you.

Each brokerage firm is allowed to set their own requirements for margin accounts, as long as they are more stringent than the requirements imposed by the Federal Reserve.

The main advantage of the margin loan is that you can use the assets in a short period of time without selling them. The interest rates may be lower than home-equity loan rates, but margin interest used for personal purposes is not tax deductible, affecting the after-tax rate. Therefore, margin loans provide an alternative short-term source of college financing.

The disadvantage to this type of loan is that if the stock price greatly declines, you may be issued a margin call, which requires you to deposit cash or more securities in the account, or the stock has to be sold.

RETIREMENT ACCOUNT LOANS

Borrowing from retirement accounts may also be considered as a source for college funding. The advantages of borrowing from these sources are a generally favorable interest rate and repayment terms, and the ease of obtaining the loan. However, if these loans are not repaid within a certain period of time, usually five years, the outstanding principal balance becomes taxable income and subject to a 10% penalty if the borrower is under age 59 1/2. Also, if the employee loses a job, the outstanding loan balance may have to be immediately repaid or taxable income occurs. In addition, the borrower gives up the ability to defer tax on the withdrawn assets and may be jeopardizing retirement savings. Furthermore, even though the retirement fund is earning interest on the college loan, it is foregoing the interest it would have earned had it been invested in a mutual fund at a possibly higher rate of return.

Some retirement plans prohibit or restrict distributions before retirement. However, hardship distributions from 401(k) plans, subject to the 10% penalty, are allowed to meet certain college expenses. Taking a hardship distribution precludes the plan participant from contributing to the plan for 12 months.

LIFE INSURANCE LOANS

Some parents use life insurance loans as a source of college funding. You should beware of taking out a life insurance loan. What typically happens when you take out a life insurance loan for a long period of time is that the loan balance increases because you do not pay the interest. Therefore, as the loan value increases, your family gets very little, if any, death benefits. Also, the loan balance can eat up all the cash value, and there is no cash left in the policy to sustain it. The policy then terminates unless you pay back the loan. If it terminates, you do not have to repay the loan plus accrued interest, but you will have to recognize the loan as taxable income.

If you are borrowing from the policy for college expenses and do not plan on repayment, you should only borrow an amount that will not terminate the policy until age 100, taking into account whether interest and premiums will be paid out-of-pocket or not. The loan is usually paid off on death, out of the proceeds. Life insurance loans can give you an option of paying for college, but you should beware of the pitfalls of borrowing too much and causing the policy to terminate.

As with retirement account loans, the true cost of the loan may be affected by the loss of investment return.

Module 3
College/Retirement Investments

Investment Factors for
College and Retirement Investments:

- Investment control
- Investment flexibility
- Rate of return versus risk
- Tax benefits and efficiency
- Financial aid opportunity
- Self-completion of the college and retirement

When developing a plan to save for retirement and college at the same time, you must use a long-term approach to develop funding plans for retirement and college. If you think only in terms of funding college, and not retirement, you may be forced to consider conservative short-term investments to meet immediate college funding needs. These conservative short-term investments may produce lower-yields during college years and the years immediately preceding college years.

If you take a holistic long-term approach to funding college and retirement at the same time, you can invest in higher-yielding investments because of the longer time frame. You will not be forced to invest in conservative short-term investments for college. The low yields of these short-term investments could have a significant negative effect on your future retirement funds.

Since there are many attractive loan programs available to you and your children to pay for college, you are not forced to use conservative short-term investments or liquidate long-term investments to pay for college costs.

INVESTMENT FACTORS TO CONSIDER
The six factors that should be evaluated when selecting college and retirement investments are:

INVESTMENT CONTROL
Direct control of the investment is important to insure keeping up with college inflation and maintaining an appropriate rate of return versus investment risk.

INVESTMENT FLEXIBILITY
The investment should be flexible enough to be used for either college or retirement funding. Flexibility to reposition the asset to a non-assessable asset for financial aid eligibility purposes is also an important consideration.

RATE OF RETURN VERSUS RISK
The investment should have a rate of return commensurate with the risk related to the investment. Usually, the higher the rate of return, the higher the investment risk and vice versa.

TAX BENEFITS AND EFFICIENCY
The "Kiddie Tax" should be avoided. Tax-deferred growth and tax-free withdrawals are desirable. Capital gain taxation versus ordinary income taxation should be considered. Coordination with the education tax incentives to maximize their benefits is an important factor. The comparison of tax benefits of the investment to its rate of return is a basic financial consideration.

EFFECT ON FINANCIAL AID
The effect of investments on eligibility for financial aid must be considered. As will be seen in the next sections, there are certain investments that have no effect or eligibility for financial aid. If financial aid eligibility is a possibility these investments must be given serious consideration.

SELF-COMPLETION OF THE COLLEGE AND RETIREMENT FUNDING PLAN
Adequate funding of the education and retirement needs, in the event of death or disability, should be a priority. If a family is concerned about self-completion of the children's education costs, the adequacy of its insurance coverage should be examined.

COLLEGE AND RETIREMENT INVESTMENTS
Following are investment options for college and retirement.

COVERDELL EDUCATION SAVINGS ACCOUNT
The Coverdell Education Savings Account (CESA) is a trust account funded by non-deductible contributions. The CESA is used to pay for future qualified education expenses of the beneficiary, the student, of the account. The CESA is exempt from income tax.

Calculation of the Contribution
The maximum contribution to a CESA is $2,000 per year per beneficiary. The contribution must be made in cash, and no contributions can be made after the beneficiary reaches 18 years of age.

Aggregate contributions for the benefit of a particular beneficiary in excess of $2,000 for a calendar year are treated as excess contributions. If the excess contributions, and any earnings attributable to them, are not withdrawn from the CESA before the tax return for the year is due, the excess contributions are subject to a 6% excise tax for each year the excess amount remains in the account.

The 6% penalty for excess contributions to a CESA can be avoided if the excess contributions, and respective earnings, are distributed to the beneficiary before the first day of the sixth month of the tax year following the year in which the contributions are made.

Maximum Lifetime Contribution Allowed
The maximum lifetime contribution that can be made for a beneficiary is $36,000, $2,000 x 18 years. Individuals may make a contribution to a CESA no later than the due date for filing the individual's income tax return. Accordingly, for 2006, the deadline for making a contribution will be April 15, 2007.

Contribution Phase-Out
Contributions to a CESA are phased out when the taxpayer reaches certain levels of modified AGI. The $2,000 limit is phased out for joint filers with modified AGI that is double the single filer phase-out amounts. Accordingly, single filers continue to phase out the contribution eligibility as modified AGI moves from $95,000 to $110,000. Joint filers phase out the contribution eligibility as modified AGI increases from $190,000 to $220,000.

> *Example: A married taxpayer with modified AGI of $205,000 could contribute a maximum of $1,000 to a CESA. Nonetheless, the beneficiary of the CESA could have other contributions to the account to bring the total to $2,000 for that year.*
>
> **Planning tip:** As a planning strategy, a taxpayer who had modified AGI in excess of the phase-out limits could gift the cash to another taxpayer, possibly a child, with modified AGI less than the phase-out limits. This taxpayer could then make the maximum contribution of $2,000 to the CESA.

Corporations and other non-individual entities, including tax-exempt organizations, are permitted to make contributions to CESAs, regardless of the income of the corporation or entity during the year of the contribution.

Distribution for Qualified Expenses
If distributions from the CESA are made for qualified education expenses, the distributions are tax-free.

Post-secondary qualified education expenses are the cost of attendance, COA, expenses at a qualified post-secondary institution. The COA consists of tuition, fees, books, supplies, equipment, room and board, only when the student is enrolled on at least a half-time basis as described for the Hope Scholarship Credit. Room and board costs can also be included to the extent of the minimum allowance for room and board costs used for federal financial aid programs. If the distribution is in excess of the qualified expenses for a particular calendar year, the excess distribution will be taxable. The taxable portion is the portion that represents earnings that have accumulated tax-free in the CESA. The taxable portion of the distribution is also subject to a 10% penalty. The penalty is waived if the beneficiary dies, is disabled, or receives a grant or scholarship that causes the qualified expenses to be less than the CESA distribution.

Qualified education expenses also include "qualified elementary and secondary school expenses," which are defined to include:

1. Expenses for tuition, fees for academic tutoring, special needs services at a public, private or religious school that provides elementary or secondary education, kindergarten through grade 12, as determined under state law.

2. Expenses for room and board, uniforms, transportation, and supplementary items and services, including extended day programs, which are required or provided by a public, private or religious school in connection with the student's enrollment or attendance.

3. Expenses for the purchase of any computer technology or equipment or Internet access or related services, if such technology, equipment or services are used by the child and the child's family during any of the years the child is in school. This definition excludes expenses for computer software designed for sports, games or hobbies unless predominantly educational in nature.

Eligible Students
To be eligible for a tax-free distribution from a CESA, the student can be enrolled on a "less than half-time" basis at a qualified post-secondary educational institution.

The student may have been convicted of a federal or state drug felony and still be an eligible student for a CESA distribution.

Interaction with Other Education Tax Benefits
A taxpayer can claim a Hope Credit or a Lifetime Learning Credit in the same year as he receives tax-free distribution from a Coverdell Education Savings Account, on behalf of the same student. The Coverdell Education Savings Account distribution, however, cannot be used for the same educational expenses.

Distribution from Both CESAs and Qualified Tuition Plans
If distributions from a CESA and a qualified tuition plan, QTP, exceed the student's qualified education expenses for the year, after reduction by amounts received as tax-free scholarships and amounts used in claiming the Hope or Lifetime Learning Credit, the student-beneficiary is required to allocate the expenses between the distributions to determine the amount of distributions included in income.

CESA Termination
The balance of a CESA must be distributed when the beneficiary becomes 30 years of age. If a CESA is terminated, without distributing all the funds in the account, the balance in the account will be subject to taxation and a 10% penalty. These tax consequences may be avoided if the account balance is "rolled over" to other members of the designated beneficiary's family. These family members include sons, daughters, brothers, sisters, nephews, nieces, certain in-laws, and any spouse of such persons.

CESA Gift Tax Considerations
Contributions to a CESA are considered gifts and thus reduce the annual $12,000 gift exclusion of the contributor.

Planning tip: If you have invested in a CESA and now find that it is counter-productive for qualifying for financial aid, you can roll the CESA, tax-free, into a QTP for the same beneficiary.

Financial Aid Consequences

The student will not have financial aid income during college years on the interest portion of any distribution from the CESA.

If the student does not withdraw the CESA funds during college years, the value of the account will be assessed as an asset of the account owner. Because of this assessment of CESAs and the effect CESAs have on the eligibility to qualify for the HC and LC, CESAs can be counter-productive for families that qualify for financial aid.

Under the Federal Methodology, a Coverdell Education Savings Account (CESA) is considered an asset of the parent. In addition, if the student's siblings have CESAs and the student is required to file the PROFILE application form, the value of the siblings' CESAs is assessed at the parents' rate.

Planning tip: Students should consider delaying the withdrawal of their CESA funds until after December 31st of their last year in college. This will not prevent the student or the parents from claiming the Hope Credit or Lifetime Learning Credit. If possible, the student should prepay the tuition and related fees for the college term that begins after December 31st and pay the balance of the college expenses after January 1st (e.g., room and board) with funds from a CESA withdrawal. This allows the student or the student's parents to claim the HC or LC for the qualified tuition and related fees paid before December 31st. The room and board, books, and other college expenses could be paid after January 1st with the CESA withdrawal.

QUALIFIED TUITION PLANS

Distributions from a state-sponsored QTP are excluded from the gross income of the student/beneficiary to the extent that the distributions are used to pay for qualified higher-education expenses.

Maximum Contribution Allowed

The maximum non-deductible contribution allowed is determined by the total qualified education expenses. Each individual state determines what this total amount will be for the QTP.

Contribution Phase-Out

There is no phase-out of the amount of contribution to a QTP due to taxpayer income levels.

Qualified Expenses

Contributions to a QTP may be made only for future qualified education expenses. Qualified higher education expenses include tuition, fees, books, supplies, equipment, and room and board. The inclusion of room and board is limited to students who will be enrolled at least half time.

Eligible Students
To have an eligible distribution from a QTP, the beneficiary can be enrolled on a less than a half-time basis. However, if a distribution for room and board is made from a QTP, then the beneficiary must be enrolled on a half or full-time basis.

Members of a family eligible for this program include sons, daughters, brothers, sisters, cousins, nephews, and nieces, as well as the spouses of such persons. The student may have been convicted of a federal or state drug felony.

QTP Gift Considerations
Contributions to a QTP are considered completed gifts from the contributor to the beneficiary. Contributions that exceed the annual gift tax exclusion limit, currently $12,000 for single parents and $24,000 for married parents who gift split, may be elected as being made ratably over the 5-year period beginning in the year the contribution is made.

> *Example: A contribution of $40,000 made to a QTP could be treated as being made over 5 years, with an $8,000 per year gift deemed to have been made by the contributor. The $8,000 gift is less than the annual gift exclusion of $12,000. Therefore, there would be no gift tax consequences to the contributor. In the event of a rollover of the QTP funds, there are no transfer tax consequences if the beneficiaries are of the same generation. If the beneficiaries are of different generations, a 5-year averaging rule may be applied to exempt up to $60,000 per contributor, or $120,000 for a married couple, of the transfer from gift tax.*

Financial Aid Consequences
QTPs are included as an asset of the parent. Also, an increasing number of colleges are considering the total distribution from a QTP to be a "resource" of the student, which will reduce the student's financial aid eligibility dollar for dollar.

A 1099-Q will be used to report distributions. Gross distributions will be reported along with the earnings portion and the portion representing basis. The recipient will have to figure out if it is taxable or exempt.

Taxable Withdrawals
To the extent the distributions from a QTP exceeds the eligible higher-education expenses, a portion of the QTP earnings is taxable.

10% Penalty on Nonqualified Distributions
A 10% penalty is imposed on the earnings portion of withdrawals that exceed the current year higher education expenditures.

Exceptions to the 10% penalty include:

1.   Distributions after the beneficiary dies or becomes disabled.

2.   Distributions as a result of the child receiving a nontaxable scholarship or similar assistance, to the extent the distribution does not exceed the amount of the scholarship or assistance.

3. Distributions caused by the reduction in "qualified education expenses" for taxpayer claiming the Hope or Lifetime Learning Credit .

Coordination with Hope and Lifetime Learning Credits
A taxpayer may claim a Hope or Lifetime Learning Credit and exclude from gross income amounts distributed from a QTP for the same year, provided that the QTP exclusion and college credit may not be claimed for the same educational expenses.

Change in Qualified Tuition Plan Beneficiary
Under present law, any amount withdrawn from a QTP and rolled over within 60 days to another QTP for a new beneficiary who is a member of the family of the old beneficiary, is not treated as a taxable distribution. Similarly, the designated beneficiary can be changed without triggering income, provided the new beneficiary is a member of the family of the old beneficiary.

Rollover to a New Section 529 Plan for the Same Beneficiary
The tax law now permits a rollover from one QTP for a designated beneficiary to another QTP for the same beneficiary, provided that there is only one such transfer or rollover within any 12-month period.

Comparison of State Tuition Plans
For an excellent comparison and recap of individual state tuition plans, **refer to** www.savingforcollege.com or 529directory.com.

EE Bonds
Ever since the U.S. government improved the return on Series EE savings bonds to enable them to compete more effectively against other financial products, they have been a convenient way to save small sums systematically for a college fund.

Tax-Free Withdrawal for College
The interest for U.S. EE Bond redemptions, used to pay for qualified education expenses, is tax-free. To qualify for the income exclusion, the bonds must be issued after December 31, 1989, and purchased by an individual who is 24 years of age or older. Bond proceeds must be used to pay qualified higher education expenses of the taxpayer, spouse, or any dependent.

If a taxpayer's redemption proceeds, interest and principal, exceed the qualified education expenses for that year, a ratable portion of the interest proceeds is taxable.

> *Example: If a taxpayer redeems $10,000, composed of $5,000 interest and $5,000 principal, and pays only $6,000 in qualified expenses, $2,000 of the interest would be taxable, $4,000 / $10,000 = 40% x $5,000 = $2,000 taxable interest.*

Phase-Out Limits
The tax-free interest is phased out when the taxpayer reaches certain levels of modified AGI. It is phased out when the modified AGI is between $63,100 and $78,100, for single or head of household taxpayers; and between $94,700 and $124,700, for married taxpayers for the year 2006. These phase-out levels are adjusted yearly for inflation.

Married taxpayers must file a joint return for the tax year in which education expenses are paid to exclude interest from Series EE Bonds.

Qualified education expenses for the purpose of this tax benefit are defined as tuition and related fees at an eligible educational institution. For tax years beginning after December 31, 1997, the transfer of bond redemption proceeds to a Qualified Tuition Program or to a CESA for the taxpayer, the taxpayer's spouse or taxpayer's dependent is considered a qualified education expense. However, the amount of tax-free interest claimed by the taxpayer will reduce the qualified expenses used in the calculation of the Hope Scholarship Credit, HC and the Lifetime Learning Credit, LC.

To be eligible for the tax-free interest benefit the student must be the taxpayer, the taxpayer's spouse, or the taxpayer's dependent, and the student must have been enrolled at an eligible institution. Married taxpayers must file a joint return to be eligible for the tax-free redemption.

I-BONDS

A family may purchase the Treasury's new "I-Bond" which provides a return that rises and falls with inflation. Only $30,000 of I-Bonds may be purchased in any calendar year. I-Bonds may be purchased from most banks, credit unions, or savings institutions.

A family may defer paying taxes on I-Bond interest, which is automatically reinvested and added to the principal. Tax reporting is similar to reporting on EE bonds; the federal tax on the interest may be deferred until the bond is redeemed or the bond reaches maturity in thirty years.

> **Planning tip:** If the I-Bond is owned by a child currently in a low tax bracket, who expects later to be in a higher tax bracket, the child may elect the accrual method of reporting the interest and pay taxes currently on the income.

As with traditional savings bonds, the I-Bond interest is exempt from state and local taxes.

> **Observation:** If the bond is redeemed to pay for college tuition or other college fees, all or part of the interest may be excludable from income if modified AGI is under an annual phase-out limit; this is the same exclusion rule as for EE Bonds used for tuition. However, this exclusion only applies if the bond is purchased by a taxpayer age 24 or older.

> *Example: A parent with high taxable income adopts the strategy of purchasing a $5,000 I-Bond annually as a gift to a child, doing so for 16 years, from age 3 to age 18 of the child, for a total investment of $80,000. Assuming that these I-Bonds averaged a 7% overall yield, and that the child cashed in the I-Bonds equally over the next four years for college costs, the average annual withdrawals would be $41,200. On average, the child would recognize $21,200 of federal taxable income per year: $164,800 total withdrawal, 4 x $41,200, less the total investment of $80,000, divided by 4 years equals average income of $21,200. This income would be taxed at 10/15% in the child's return, and annually could be offset by education tax*

credits of $1,500 to $2,000. There would be no state or local tax on these earnings.

TRADITIONAL IRAS

The $4,000 deduction of a traditional IRA can shelter the investment income of a student in pre-college years, assuming the student has wages or other earned income at least equal to the IRA amount. This strategy has the effect of deferring other investment income to college years. The student then withdraws the IRA to pay college tuition, and uses education credits to offset the tax on the IRA withdrawal.

An exception exists to the 10% early withdrawal penalty for IRA withdrawals when the distribution is used to pay for qualified higher education expenses. Qualified education expenses include tuition, fees, books, supplies and equipment. Room and board are also included if the student is enrolled on at least a half-time basis. These education expenses must be reduced by any tax-free scholarships or grants, qualified U.S. Series EE Bond, veterans' education benefits, and other tax-free educational benefits.

To be eligible for the penalty-free IRA distribution the student must be the taxpayer, the taxpayer's spouse, or any child or grandchild of the taxpayer or the taxpayer's spouse. The distribution must be used to pay for qualified education expenses. Tax-free distributions from a CESA, qualified U.S. EE Savings Bond, or employer-provided educational assistance will reduce the amount of qualified education expenses for the penalty-free IRA distribution.

> *Example: Larry is a dependent on his parents' tax return during his high school years. During these years, a traditional IRA is used to reduce Larry's taxable income to zero each year. Upon entering college, Larry claims himself as a dependent because he provides over one-half of his own support by paying tuition and room and board from his own funds. Assume that Larry's $7,000 of IRA contributions have appreciated to $9,000, including $2,000 of earnings, by the time he enters college. The following chart summarizes the tax treatment over his last four high school years.*

Student Status	Dependent			Not Dependent	
Year in School	Grade 9	Grade 10	Grade 11	Grade 12	College
Wages	$ 1,500	$ 3,000	$ 4,000	$ 4,000	$ 4,500
Interest/Dividends/CG	1,500	2,000	2,250	2,250	3,000
IRA	(1,250)	(1,750)	(2,000)	(2,000)	9,000
Personal Exemption					(3,300)
Std. Deduction	(1,750)	(3,250)	(4,250)	(4,250)	(5,150)
Taxable income	---0----	---0---	---0---	---0---	$ 8,050
Tax					$ 830
Hope Credit					(830)
Total Tax Paid	---0---	---0---	---0---	---0---	---0---

Effectively, Larry has managed to avoid tax on his investment income during his high school years through the use of a deductible IRA, and then later is able to avoid all tax and penalty on the IRA withdrawal through the use of the education credits.

Planning tip: As shown in the previous example, a traditional IRA can be withdrawn penalty-free and possibly tax-free to pay for college costs. Alternatively, if the IRA funds are not needed for college, a student can elect to convert to a Roth IRA during college years. The Hope Scholarship Credit, HC, or Lifetime Learning Credit, LC, may offset the taxable income generated by the conversion.

ROTH IRAS
A Roth IRA may be a good college investment option.

The advantages are:
1.   A Roth IRA is a non-assessable asset in the EFC computation.

2.   The earnings on a Roth IRA grow tax-free.

3.   Withdrawal from a Roth IRA will not affect eligibility to claim the Hope Credit or Lifetime Learning Credit, nor will it reduce the "qualified education expenses" for the student loan interest tax deduction.

4.   There is no taxability of withdrawals of contributions if used for non-college purposes.

5.   With proper tax planning, the child may be able to contribute $4,000 annually to his own Roth IRA

   Example: Jack and Jill operate a sole-proprietor business. Their ten-year-old child, Ryne, worked in the business on weekends and during his summer school break. Ryne was paid $4,000 per year for this work. The parents received a tax deduction for these wages and because Ryne was under 18 years of age, they were not required to withhold Social Security payroll taxes on these wages. Since Ryne dreamed of going to college, he invested the $4,000 in a Roth IRA to help cover his future college costs. In addition to the $4,000 Ryne invested, his parents contributed an additional $4,000 each to their own Roth IRA, which can also eventually be used for future college costs, for a total of $12,000 per year.

If the child were to have more funds than needed for college, the Roth IRA may be used in lieu of funding additional QTP amounts. The Roth IRA does not need to be consumed for college as do QTP amounts, but has essentially the same tax result.

Investment income from Roth contributions is also tax-free if they are held for five years and the IRA owner is age 59½ or older when distributions begin. With regular IRAs, the income is only tax-deferred.

TAX-EFFICIENT FUNDS

Typically, tax-efficient stock funds buy and hold stocks for the long term. As a result, they do not distribute capital gains at the end of the year. They also avoid high-dividend yielding stocks to limit taxable income.

A tax-efficient stock fund may use some or all of the following strategies:

1. "Indexing" is when an investor invests in index funds that buy and hold a portfolio of stocks tied to a specific benchmark, such as the S & P 500. Index funds are tax-efficient because their trading decisions are relatively predictable. As shareholder money flows in, an index fund buys stocks to track its benchmark index and the fund sells stocks as investors redeem shares.

2. Investing in low-portfolio-turnover stock funds can increase tax efficiency. These funds typically invest in undervalued stocks and hold on to them for at least five years.

3. "Tax-wise accounting" is a tax-friendly technique used by most tax-efficient fund managers. When a stock is sold, a tax-efficient manager earmarks the highest-cost shares for first sale. This course of action either minimizes the gain or increases the loss realized on the stock.

4. "Harvesting" is a procedure that involves deliberately selling securities on which a portfolio has a loss. That loss can then be used to offset gains on other securities now, or in the future.

   Note: Exchange Traded Funds, ETFs, are index-based equity instruments that represent ownership in either a fund or a unit investment trust and give investors the opportunity to buy and sell shares of an entire stock portfolio as a single security. They have low expense ratios, are simple to use and explain, and are more tax-efficient than index funds. ETFs are not subject to shareholder redemptions so they don't have to sell off their holdings and realize gains.

ANNUITIES

These types of investments are primarily effective for people who will be over age 59½ when education costs are incurred. Although annuities can be successfully used as an exempt asset for financial aid purposes, shortfalls associated with these investments for college include:

1. Annuities are taxed as ordinary income.

2. Transfers or gifts, other than to a spouse, trigger a taxable event.

3. There are withdrawal or surrender penalties. Most annuities have considerable withdrawal or surrender penalties for the first 5-10 years or more. This penalty is on the *entire amount* of the annuity, not just the appreciation, and is usually associated with sales commissions.

4. There are additional fees for mortality and risk expense. In addition to the normal investment fees, annuities contain a "mortality and risk" expense to cover the

insurance obtained. However, this insurance covers only the original investment. If the annuity account is less than the original investment and the account holder dies, the insurance covers only the difference. If the annuity account has grown and the account holder dies, the insurance pays nothing.

5. There is a 10% penalty if withdrawn before age 59½. Unless an exception applies, the earnings portion of a withdrawal from an annuity will be subject to a 10% tax penalty if withdrawn by the annuitant before age 59½.

   Note: Variable annuities, a mutual fund-type annuity, are attractive to some families as a way to save for college. The advantages of this type of investment are their tax-deferral of earnings and ability to keep up with the high inflation rates of college.

UNIVERSAL LIFE INSURANCE

Some families may find life insurance an attractive way to save for college. The advantages of this type of investment are:

1. Life insurance is not assessed in the EFC calculation at most colleges.

2. The tax-deferred growth of earnings is an advantage.

3. There is an availability of low-interest loans from the policy during college years.

4. The insurance coverage of the future cost of college in the event of death.

5. The coverage of the future cost of college in the event of disability, if the policy has a disability insurance feature.

6. There is a possible protection from creditor claims.

Universal life insurance policies can serve a dual purpose for college fund investors:

1. These policies provide the parents of dependent children with the security of insurance and a way to build up assets by disciplined savings.

2. Universal life provides fairly priced *lifetime* insurance coverage for the parents and accumulates value to tap for retirement income later in life.

The cash value of an insurance policy is its college investment component. The premium, paid by the parents, is applied to three areas:

1. A mortality charge to fund the pure insurance, based on the insured person's age, sex and health.

2. Commissions and administrative fees.

3. An investment account, which builds cash value for the policy owner.

By tradition, insurance companies have been fairly conservative investors and developed policies in which cash value builds up at rates comparable to that of other conservative investment alternatives, such as CDs.

The special feature of most universal life policies is that they are flexible. You can generally suspend premium payments for a time or increase the premiums to build up cash value more quickly, borrow against cash value or make partial withdrawals. They can adapt to the differing insurance needs the parents may experience at various stages in life, including the period when you are building up a college fund. Like most life insurance, universal life enjoys special status under current tax laws. Death benefits are *not* taxed to the recipients. The cash value increases on a tax-deferred basis, which means that earned interest is not currently taxed.

VARIABLE UNIVERSAL LIFE

The Variable Universal Life, VUL, can provide parents with an alternative for paying college costs. Not only does it provide control, wide investment selection, tax-free growth and tax-free withdrawals, but it also allows parents to pay for college without having to deplete their retirement savings. Better still, the policy provides the security of a policy death benefit to pay for college. In addition, making the premium payments on permanent life insurance is a forced savings. Most parents will not want to lapse the policy by not making the premium payments.

If parents continue to make deposits to a VUL, when the time comes to pay the college bills, they can easily withdraw money from the contract, either as a cost-basis withdrawal or a wash loan on a tax-free basis.

CASH -VALUE LIFE INSURANCE

Cash-value life insurance can be an effective addition to your college fund if the insurance is needed. So the first step is to assess the need, or identify a possible insurance gap. This can be done using the following simple procedure:

1.   Estimate the annual expense of maintaining the family's current standard of living.

2.   Estimate the household income following the death of a major provider.

3.   Estimate the income that could reasonably be generated by investing the lump sums payable to family survivors from pension and profit-sharing plans and existing life insurance policies.

4.   If there is a gap between estimated expenses and income, adding additional life insurance as part of the overall college funding plan should be considered.

Also, it must be decided whether to fill an insurance gap by buying term insurance or cash-value life insurance. If the gap between the household's expenses and its income after the loss of a major provider is substantial, especially during the child's college years, a five-year term policy to cover the extraordinary expenses during that period could be the most economical choice.

Chapter 3
Steps to Save for College and Retirement

SAVING FOR COLLEGE AND RETIREMENT

As you can see, saving for college and retirement can be a daunting task. You may be unable to fund both simultaneously without sacrificing your current lifestyle. If this is the case, you must choose your investment goal. Retirement funding should take priority.

However, since college is a more immediate problem and involves your children, you may fund college at the expense of your retirement. This can lead to disastrous retirement consequences. Therefore, unless you are secure in your retirement plan, you should not consider saving for your children's college costs. The children can borrow for the entire cost of college and not jeopardize your retirement. You may not be able to borrow for your retirement.

DETERMINATION OF RETIREMENT FINANCIAL NEEDS
You will probably need to plan on living on less money in retirement. But the good news is that you may be able to reduce many of your expenses. For instance, you may need to maintain only one car and may have a smaller or no mortgage payment. In these ways, as well as many others, you can reduce expenses.

Set the goal of initially having a minimum of 70% to 75% of your pre-retirement income coming in at retirement.

Make adjustments gradually rather than suddenly. With this in mind, start living on less beginning 3 to 5 years prior to retirement. Finding corners that can be cut, without reducing the quality of life, can be a challenging, but very rewarding, adventure in pre-retirement planning.

PROJECTION OF RETIREMENT INCOME
Generally, retirement income will consist of your Social Security benefits, your pension and/or retirement savings plan benefits, interest and dividend income from personal savings, and post-retirement earnings.

If you have a company-sponsored retirement plan, they can help you estimate projected benefits from your retirement plans. You may find that during the "empty nest" years, you are able to contribute substantially to your retirement savings.

Your Social Security Office can assist you in estimating your future Social Security benefits. You should check the accuracy of your Social Security income records every 3 years. By calling the Social Security Administration number (1-800-772-1213), you may request a form to check your record at no charge.

You also will want to check carefully with the Social Security office to determine the amount of income you may earn after retirement without jeopardizing your Social Security benefits.

Some families are fortunate enough to have extra sources of personal income. These may have come from an inheritance or from personal savings and may consist of investments in stocks, bonds, real estate, and other assets. All of these need to be figured into your retirement planning schedule.

If your planning indicates a significant difference between retirement needs and retirement income, you need to plan carefully how you are going to cope with the shortfall. If the gap is too large, you or your spouse may need to continue working, at least on a part-time basis, beyond the time of your retirement

HANDLING UNFORESEEN EMERGENCY EXPENSES
Sadly, many of you will face a financial emergency in your retirement years. As preparation, you should attempt to have an emergency fund in an interest-bearing account that is readily accessible to you. You should firmly commit that these funds are only for a *real* emergency. Small consumer loans and credit cards may be convenient sources of emergency funds, but they carry a very high cost. An adequate emergency fund can eliminate the additional expense of interest. Use this fund only as "a last resort" and make every effort to replenish it after it has been accessed.

EFFECTS OF INFLATION
Inflation is a significant problem for anyone on fixed incomes, because purchasing power diminishes as prices rise. Although Social Security has a built-in cost-of-living factor, its future may be in doubt in light of federal deficits and future Social Security tax increases to support the system.

Long-term inflationary trends are very difficult to project, but we cannot ignore them. The best approach is to put aside as much money as possible before you retire. It is also important that the earnings or returns on your invested assets be greater than inflation. Otherwise, the real value of the investment declines. Few families have ever indicated that they had "too much" retirement income.

PROJECTION OF LIVING EXPENSES FOR RETIREMENT
First, establish a budget and develop a record keeping system now. This will help you know how you are spending your current income and will help you discover expenses that you can reduce after you retire. You may even find funds now that could be saved to help with your retirement funding later.

INSURANCE NEEDS AFTER RETIREMENT
Insurance needs change significantly with age. In the health arena, surveys confirm that many retirees worry about having a major illness with adequate hospitalization benefits. You need to understand that Medicare provides both hospitalization insurance and medical insurance. The medical insurance portion is optional and, if you choose, you may pay a monthly premium for it to Social Security. Medicare does not pay for everything and the plan has undergone, and will continue to undergo, many changes.

Many private insurance companies offer "Medigap" policies that supplement Medicare. Congress has established federal standards for such policies. In most states, you may choose from a standard list of ten Medigap packages. Of course, the more comprehensive packages cost more. Be informed and shop carefully. You should explore the offerings of different insurance companies to make the best choice at the best price for your specific needs.

Life insurance needs may change drastically with retirement. At retirement, your primary purpose for purchasing life insurance no longer exists. You no longer have to worry about protecting your dependent survivors from the loss of income between the time of your death and the time your income would have ceased at retirement. However, if you want to leave an estate to your heirs, life insurance may be a viable solution for this desire.

Carefully evaluate whole life insurance policies that you may have taken out long before retirement. Check to see if the policy's monthly premiums must be paid until death, or if the policy could be converted to a paid-up policy with no future obligations. Also check to see if the policy has accumulated dividends that could be withdrawn to meet retirement needs. In addition, if substantial cash values are built up in the policy, you may withdraw these on a tax-free basis to supplement your retirement income. Continuing to pay large insurance premiums during retirement years can drain your available finances significantly and unnecessarily.

Carefully rethink your insurance needs, perhaps with the assistance of a trusted insurance advisor. This is an important part of your retirement financial planning.

RESPONSIBILITY OF RETIREMENT PLANNING
By answering these questions, you can plan and anticipate a meaningful period of life after your active years. Planning comes right down to you as an individual. No one will do the planning for you. You must do it yourself. Planning is a process that should be ongoing. You and your spouse should review your plan frequently to determine how well you are meeting your plan's objectives and to revise those objectives in light of your real life situation.

Proper financial planning for retirement may seem like a major task, and it certainly is. But then, nearly 30% of one's lifetime may be spent after retirement, and doesn't 30% of your life deserve adequate planning?

COLLEGE SAVINGS ARE BASED ON RETIREMENT ADEQUACY

The amount saved for college is dependent on the adequacy of your retirement plan. If you are on track to meet your retirement goals, you can then start investing for your children's education costs. If you are not on track to fund your retirement, you should not invest for education costs. The education costs can be covered by loans in your children's names or, as a last choice, in your names.

Saving for college and saving for retirement are somewhat mutually exclusive. You cannot use the same dollars twice.

Does this prevent you from saving for education costs and your retirement at the same time? The answer is absolutely not!

There is no do-it-yourself Turbo Tax® for college financial planning. You need a professional who knows the rules. There is simply too much money at risk for you to learn this process by trial and error. Even if you hear from a well-intentioned but misinformed guidance counselor or neighbor that you don't need to pay money to a professional college financial advisor, you may cost yourself thousands of dollars if you try to do it yourself. College is one of your single biggest investments. College funding laws and strategies change each year. A professional college financial advisor can maximize your eligibility for financial aid and education tax incentives, keep you informed, give you direction, answer your questions, and complete the paperwork in a timely manner.

In order to insure a coordinated implementation of a college and retirement funding plan, each person involved in the plan should be assigned duties. Deadlines for completing these duties should be set to insure timely completion of the plan. You should monitor and update the progress of the plan to insure its success.

Since the college funding process can encompass many months or years, you should keep yourself informed on new laws and strategies. This can be accomplished with a periodic newsletter or through college discussion boards provided by financial professionals.

The following steps can be implemented to save and pay for college and retirement at the same time without sacrificing your current lifestyle or going broke!

Steps to Solving the College and Retirement Dilemma

13 Steps to Solving the Dilemma...

Step #1   **Project future retirement**
cost based on your retirement age
and annual amount desired
in retirement years

Now that you have completed your education funding plan, you must consider your retirement funding plan.

The first step in this process is to determine your total retirement cost.

To determine this cost you will have to determine your desired annual retirement amount. You will have to project what amount will be needed at your retirement age to fund this annual retirement amount.

13 Steps to Solving the Dilemma...

Step #2   **Determine what funds are currently available for your retirement**

Next, you will have to determine what funds are currently available for future retirement costs.

The future value of these funds will have to be projected at a certain rate of return to determine what will be available at the time of your retirement.

13 Steps to Solving the Dilemma...

**Step #3   Determine the amount of shortfall
                 in your retirement plan**

You must then determine the projected shortage in your retirement funding plan. The shortage is the difference between Step #1 and Step #2.

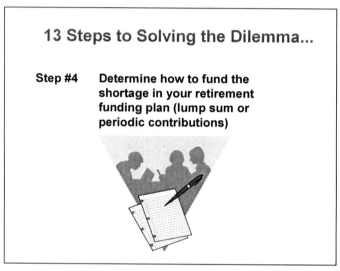

13 Steps to Solving the Dilemma...

Step #4 **Determine how to fund the shortage in your retirement funding plan (lump sum or periodic contributions)**

After the projected shortage has been determined, you must decide how you are going to fund the shortage.

You can fund the shortage with either a lump sum contribution or periodic contributions.

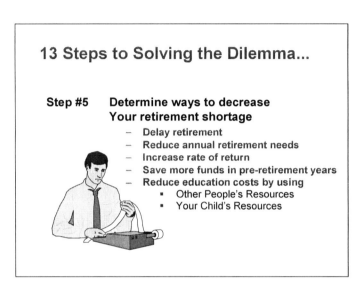

13 Steps to Solving the Dilemma...

Step #5   **Determine ways to decrease Your retirement shortage**

- Delay retirement
- Reduce annual retirement needs
- Increase rate of return
- Save more funds in pre-retirement years
- Reduce education costs by using
  - Other People's Resources
  - Your Child's Resources

If it is determined that there is a shortage in your retirement fund, you must decide if any of the following are viable options to reduce the shortage:

- Delay your retirement in order to accumulate more funds and reduce the amount needed for retirement.

- You can reduce your desired annual retirement income so that the total amount needed for retirement is reduced.

- You can try to achieve a better rate of return on your retirement investments in pre-retirement years in order to accumulate more funds.

- You can save more funds in pre-retirement years by reducing discretionary expenses or by debt consolidation.

- You can reduce your education costs. Please refer to Step #11 for options to reduce your education costs by using Other People's Resources and your Child's Resources.

13 Steps to Solving the Dilemma...

Step #6   **Select the appropriate retirement investments for funds generated in Step #4**

The last step in the retirement funding process is to select the appropriate retirement investments to invest the funds generated in Step #4.

There are several retirement investment options that could be considered, such as 401(k)s, 403(b)s, IRAs, Roth IRAs, or annuities.

You must know the pros and cons of each type of investment in order to select the appropriate investment or combination of investments.

Investments for Retirement
Since funding the parents' retirement should be the first priority, the parents should contribute to a 401(k) plan to at least take full advantage of any employer match. If the parents feel secure with their funding for retirement, they can borrow from the plan for college. Also remember, retirement accounts will not affect their children's financial aid eligibility.

If the parents do not have 401(k) plans available to them, they should consider other types of qualified retirement plans such as, 403(b) plans, Keogh plans, SEP plans, and the various IRA plans. If a 401(k) plan is available, the parents should utilize these types of retirement plans, only after they have maximized their 401(k) plans because of the 401(k) loan features and employer match.

After the parents have maximized their qualified retirement plans, they should look at non-qualified retirement funding plans such as non-qualified deferred compensation plans, annuities, and life insurance. Some of these investments have loan features that can be utilized for college funding and they probably will not affect the children's eligibility for financial aid.

13 Steps to Solving the Dilemma...

Step #7   **Project the amount of funds that will be needed for your future education costs.**

The first step is to project the total amount that will be needed for future education costs. These costs include the college and K-12 costs for all of your children.

In order to arrive at this total cost you will need to project current education costs to the point in time when you will start incurring these costs.

Remember, college costs are rising at two to three times the average inflation rate.

13 Steps to Solving the Dilemma...

Step #8   **Determine what funds are currently available to meet your education costs**

Next, you will have to determine what funds are currently available for future education costs.

The future value of these funds will have to be projected at a certain rate of return to determine what will be available at the time they are needed for education costs.

13 Steps to Solving the Dilemma...

Step #9   **Determine the shortfall in your education funding plan**

You must then determine the shortage in your education funding plan. The shortage is the difference between Step #7 and Step #8.

13 Steps to Solving the Dilemma...

Step #10   **Determine how much you need to fund the shortfall in your education funding plan (lump sum or periodic contributions)**

After the projected shortage has been determined, you must decide how you are going to fund the shortage.

You can either fund the shortage with a lump sum or periodic contributions.

13 Steps to Solving the Dilemma . . .

**Step #11   Determine how you want to fund
education costs**

- **Other People's Resources**
- **Child's Resources**
- **Your Resources**

Determine how you want to fund education costs by using the following resource:

- Other People's Resources
- Child's Resources
- Your Resources

Step #12   **Select the appropriate education investments for the funds generated in Step #10**

The last step in the education funding process is to select the appropriate education investments to invest the funds generated in Step #10.

There are several education investment options that could be considered, such as Coverdell Education Savings Accounts, Qualified Tuition Plans, or tax-efficient mutual funds.

You must know the pros and cons of each type of investment in order to select the appropriate investment or combination of investments.

Investments for Education
In order to select the appropriate investments for the education funding plan, the children's eligibility to receive financial aid should be considered.

If the children are expected to be eligible for financial aid, investments that will not reduce their financial aid eligibility should first be considered. These types of investments would include retirement accounts, annuities, and life insurance. If other types of investments are selected, the investment should be held in the name of the parents because of their lower financial aid asset assessment rate.

If the children are not expected to be eligible for financial aid, the Coverdell Education Savings Account, CESA, should be the first choice since it can be used for either K-12 expenses or college expenses. It also offers the parents direct control of the investment and the flexibility of being eligible to be rolled over to a Qualified Tuition Plan, QTP, at a later date.

After the CESA has been funded, the QTP should be considered as a college funding vehicle. If there is a state tax incentive for contributing to these plans, the parents should fund the QTP to the level needed to take advantage of the state tax incentive. However, because of the harsh tax treatment of QTP withdrawals not used for college (ordinary tax rates and 10% penalty on the earnings portion of withdrawals not used for college), the parents should not over-fund a QTP. They may want to contribute only enough to cover the cost of a public college education for their children.

The final level of college funding for children that are not expected to be eligible for financial aid should be into tax-deferred investments. Suitable investments include tax-efficient funds, Series EE Bonds, I-Bonds, municipal bonds, and real estate. If the parents want to keep control of the investments, the investments should be titled in the parent's name. In order to maximize the children's lower tax bracket and the education tax incentives, the parents should gift these assets to the children and let the children liquidate the assets. If control of the investment is not an issue for the parents, the investments can be held in the name of the children via custodial or trust accounts. This will enable the family to maximize the children's lower tax bracket and the education tax incentives. However, proper tax planning must be done to avoid the "Kiddie Tax" during ages 0 – 13.

13 Steps to Solving the Dilemma...

Step #13   **Determine the amount of insurance required for self-completion of your education and retirement funding plans**

In order to insure self-completion of your education and retirement funding plans, you must consider the adequacy of your insurance coverage in the following areas:

- Do you have adequate life insurance coverage to pay for education and retirement costs in the event of an untimely death?

- Do you have adequate disability insurance coverage to pay for education and retirement costs in the event of disability?

- Do you have adequate long-term care insurance to pay for nursing home costs that could destroy your education and retirement funds?

- Do you have adequate medical insurance coverage to pay for medical expenses that could destroy both your education and retirement funds?

APPENDIX A
POSITIONING THE STUDENT TO RECEIVE MERIT AID

What is "positioning the student" or "student marketability" anyway? Why is it so important?

The fact is that one of the best ways to make college an affordable reality is by receiving tuition reductions that will mean less of a financial burden for you and your family. See Appendix D. The best way to receive tuition reductions from the colleges is for the applicant to be the kind of student and individual that the colleges are actively recruiting for their campus. Keep in mind that tuition reductions are not certainties, and every college or university will have their own particular qualities that they are seeking. Students that want to be considered for a reduction in tuition must position themselves. There are many ways to market or position your student properly, but all the methods should contain the following seven factors:

1. Good grades
2. Good SAT/ACT test scores
3. A solid resume of achievement
4. Apply early in the academic year
5. Apply to schools that recruit the same students
6. Apply to schools that have a low yield factor
7. Apply to 6-8 colleges

Good Grades
Good grades are self-explanatory. The presumption is that good grades in high school will mean good grades in college and, ultimately, graduating from college and becoming an alumnus. A student should have a minimum of a 3.0 GPA in high school to be in the running for a tuition reduction. See Appendices B and C.

SAT/ACT Test Scores
The SAT/ACT college prep test scores are merely qualifiers, but colleges have no other way to compare the academic abilities of a student from Ohio with a student from California. A student should have a minimum of 24 ACT or 1250 SAT (verbal and math) test score to be in the running for a tuition reduction. See Appendix B.

The good colleges are getting more and more competitive. If they receive applications from two students with the exact same grades and similar extra-curricular activities, they will rely on other factors to make their choice. SAT scores will be one of the other factors. Sometimes a higher SAT score can make all the difference between getting into an "O.K." school and a prestigious university.

Have Your Child Take A Good Test Preparation Course To Get A Better SAT Score
The small investment you make in a good test preparation service will pay off in high returns for your child. See Appendix B.

Solid Resume Of Achievement

During the junior and senior years, the student should build a solid resume of achievements that will imply to the college that he or she is an all-around good student, and active in student affairs, other than studies. This should be treated exactly the same as preparing a resume for a job. Send a resume with the application to each school. See Appendices B and C.

Apply Early In The Academic Year

Apply to the various colleges early in your senior year of high school (September-December). The earlier, the better! Remember, once a particular school begins to fill the following year's freshman class, the opportunity to receive a tuition reduction diminishes.

Apply To Schools That Recruit The Same Students

Private colleges that compete with each other for the same students are more likely to give a significant discount if they know the student is also applying to the competition.

Planning Tip: If the student wishes to attend a particular Catholic school, he should also apply to other Catholic schools within a radius of 200 miles. The student can also achieve the same effect by applying to other colleges in the same academic or athletic division or conference, as the college the student wishes to attend.

Apply To Schools That Have A Low Yield Factor

$$\text{Yield} = \frac{\text{Number of students actually enrolled}}{\text{Number of students admitted}}$$

Enrollment is key to a college's survival. Many colleges select students for admission to their school, only to have them enroll in another. The college has a constant battle to fill seats every year and lesser-known private colleges are even more challenged because they must compete with the low cost of public universities and the popularity of the elite private (Ivy League) schools. As a result, the lower the college's yield percentage, the higher the student's probability of receiving a tuition reduction.

Apply to 6-8 Colleges

The student should apply to 6-8 colleges, of which at least 4 represent private colleges that are in competition with the college of his choice. Applying to several colleges gives the student the opportunity to receive a tuition reduction from one college, and use that discount to ask for a similar or better award from the college of his choice. Pick an assortment of "safety schools", "competitive schools", and "reach schools". We cannot stress this point often enough, and it is important that you do this in order to greatly increase your chances of saving money by receiving tuition discounts.

Try to pick at least several schools where your child lies in the top 25% of the incoming freshman class. Otherwise, there is a good likelihood that the schools will not give you a good financial aid package, since your child will not be a desirable candidate.

APPENDIX B
ACADEMIC FACTORS AND ADMISSIONS

Most Important Tests For Admissions

Standardized tests are the most important (and feared) tests that a college-bound student faces because they figure so heavily in the college's acceptance standards. Whether these tests demonstrate a true aptitude for college success is the subject of much debate. However, the colleges do weigh these tests heavily and it is important for each student to achieve the highest possible test score. While many seek the services of private test preparation firms, there are some basic strategies that can enable students to dramatically improve their results.

Students preparing to go to college should be aware that more schools have an entrance requirement of one (or more) standardized test(s) in order to qualify for admission. Each college has its own specific policy as to when test(s) are required. The two major tests are the ACT and SAT I.

American College Test (ACT)

The ACT is a four-part, two hour and forty minute test measuring skills in English, Math, Natural Sciences and Social Studies and a twenty-five minute Profile Section indicating grades, background and achievements. The ACT should be taken at the end of the student's high school junior year and/or early in the senior year in order to meet the deadlines of many college scholarship programs.

Scholastic Aptitude Test (SAT I)

In March 2005, the SAT will undergo its most sweeping changes in recent memory. High school students entering college as early as 2006 will encounter a brand new Writing section, more advanced Math questions, and a revamped scoring system. The first to take the new SAT will be the graduating class of 2006. These students will take the new PSAT/ NMSQT in fall 2004, and the new SAT will begin to be administered in spring 2005.

The new SAT will not be harder but will be much different from the current SAT. For instance, students who do not like analogies will be happy to find out that this section of the SAT has been removed. However, the math section will now include Algebra II problems. In addition, a new writing component has been added, meaning that the SAT will now have three separate scores on the famous 200 to 800 scale: one for math, one for critical reading, and one for writing. This means the perfect 1600 no longer applies; the new perfect score is 2400.

Instead of only two scored sections, the essay will also be scored using the similar scale of 200-800 points. This changes the potential score to 2400 instead of the old score of 1600. The writing will have two subscores—a multiple-choice subscore on a scale of 20-80 and an essay subscore of 2-12. The new SAT will last a total of 3 hours and 35 minutes.

Starting in fall 2004 the PSAT will include some changes much like those made to the SAT. It will not, however, include an essay section. The fee for the new SAT will increase by $10 to $12.

The SAT II

Where the SAT I is an aptitude test, the SAT II is a subject (knowledge-based) test, on which the highly selective schools (Ivy League) place equal weight.

These subject tests are true equalizers in the admissions process and showcase the student's academic talent against the national pool of candidates. Although there are approximately twenty different SAT II tests, most selective schools require only three subject tests for admissions. The big difference among these tests is each SAT II lasts only one hour, covers a very narrow range of material, and is even easier to prepare for in advance.

Preparation For Tests

There will be some changes in the SAT starting in March 2005. The changes are manageable, they won't make the test any harder. For example, for the first time, the SAT will include a written essay to show how well the student can do the kind of writing that colleges require.

There are seven strategic steps that a student can take to properly prepare for both the ACT and SAT tests. Following these simple steps is the easiest way to achieve the highest possible score.

Step 1. The student should review the ACT/SAT I standardized tests and each college's requirements for admissions application.

Step 2. The student should get a **real** ACT/SAT I test from the guidance office and become familiar with the format and procedures. The student can use this test to examine how it looks, what it consists of and review the difficult (and time consuming) directions.

Step 3. The student should take the practice ACT/SAT I test using the official timing procedure to achieve an accurate result. This procedure can only be effective if the student obtains a real test and uses the official time limits for testing. The new SAT will feature a writing section including a short essay that requires them to take a position on an issue and use reasoning and examples to support their position. The essay will always be the first section students take on the new SAT. They'll have 25 minutes to work on the essay. The essay counts for only 30 percent of the writing section score.

The student should practice writing the essay with a time limit of 25 minutes. They may also ask their teacher for help practicing the new SAT essay.

Step 4. The student can then diagnose their weakest skills by pinpointing the problem area(s) and analyzing their weakest area(s) of knowledge.

Step 5. The student can rework the wrong answers on the original sample test, recognize the original errors and understand why they were made. The student can remedy these errors with additional work skills in weak areas. The best way for the student to prepare for the new critical reading section (currently known as Verbal) is by reading as much as possible and working hard in English class.

Step 6.   The student should prepare to take both the ACT and SAT I tests twice; once, as a high school junior, and once as a senior. This will ensure the student the highest possible score.

Step 7.   The student should take four to six SAT II tests because the college will only take the three best. These tests should be taken at the end of each year, preferably immediately after completing the subject class.

Successful completion of these seven steps will allow the student to dramatically improve the test scores and increase the student's opportunity of being admitted to the college of choice.

> **Planning Tip:** In 1998, the College Board (sponsor of the SAT II and Advanced Placement tests) developed a new, "online" service called EssayPrep. For a fee ($38 per essay review), the actual essay graders for the SAT offer advice to students for improving their writing skills. Critics of this new service say the new service allows students to be measured on their ability to pay for coaching, not their intelligence. Regardless, SAT results weigh heavily in the admissions decision and using EssayPrep would be a prudent decision for students applying to highly selective colleges. EssayPrep can be reached at www.collegeboard.org.

Admissions Is Big Business

As a parent with a child planning to attend college, the enormous process called "admissions" is inevitable. Today's college admissions process is big business and the stakes for ambitious youngsters is higher than ever. However, applying and being accepted to a college does not have to be such a painful event. Except for the Ivy League, and a handful of other very selective schools, colleges today admit a much higher ratio of applicants. Even the most prestigious colleges are spending huge sums to market themselves to prospective students.

> **Planning Tip**: If possible, the student should submit the application for admission as soon as possible in the senior year of high school. Colleges want to complete their enrollment quotas as early as possible. In order to achieve this, they sometimes give scholarships or tuition discounts to the students who apply early. They hope that these incentives will entice the student to enroll at the college.

Admission Guidelines And Strategies

The secret is understanding where the student stands in advance with a particular college. Students who understand the ins and outs of the admissions process can be very selective about the college they wish to attend. The following are some basic guidelines and strategies that can dramatically improve the student's chance of a successful admissions campaign.

Important Factors For College Admissions

There are ten important factors that colleges consider for admissions:

#1	A challenging high school curriculum.	Many AP and honors classes as well as electives that "round" the student out.
#2	Grades that reflect the student's dedication.	Many A's, although slightly lower grades in more advanced classes are preferred over "easy A" classes.
#3	A well-written essay that shares the applicant's insight, values, and goals.	Always constructed correctly and free of grammatical errors, the essay should be personal and thoughtful.
#4	A true commitment and involvement in a few activities demonstrating leadership and initiative.	Depth, not breadth, of experience is most important.
#5	Solid standardized test scores.	SAT, ACT & other test scores should be consistent with academic performance.
#6	Special talents or unique qualities that will add to the student body.	Colleges want diverse, strong student bodies for their campus.
#7	Strong letter(s) of recommendation.	Letters from teachers and guidance counselors should reflect the student's integrity, positive skills, and positive attributes.
#8	Enthusiastic interview.	No matter how good the student looks to the colleges, the colleges want enthusiasm for attending their specific school.
#9	Out of school experiences that demonstrate responsibility, dedication, and development of areas of interest.	Work, community service, meaningful use of free time; anything to show maturity.
#10	Supplemental letters of recommendation from others who have had direct knowledge and contact with the student.	Letters from coaches, employers, long-term volunteer contacts should be used over friends and family.

There are categories of students that receive special consideration for admissions approval. Some of these categories are:

- Athletics
- Special Talents
- Legacies
- VIPs
- Minorities
- Faculty/Trustee Recommendations

Admission Tools

The following strategic tools can help students through the admissions process and achieve the ultimate goal of being accepted to the college of choice:

1. Admission Application And Campaign

- Apply early. Begin completing the college admission applications either on-line or on paper. Request admission applications from colleges that the student may have added to their list and make photocopies so they'll have copies to practice on.

- Make certain the student has all the important dates/deadlines regarding the current information about the colleges that interest them.

- Complete the admission application personal statement/essay. Have the student's parents and advisers review and critique it.

- Take the SAT I & II (or ACT) and have the student's scores sent to the colleges on their list.

- Be certain the student's grade transcripts are being sent to the colleges on their list.

- If the student is applying for financial aid and has not yet completed the Financial Aid PROFILE, the student should complete it as instructed and send it in by the deadline listed.

- Complete and send in the FAFSA, using estimated numbers if necessary (changes can always be made later). Make certain the student and their parents have sent all required information to the financial aid office at each college.

- Make certain the student's applications have been received by the colleges. The student should receive an acknowledgment; if they do not, call or e-mail the college.

- Take a tour of the college and surrounding area and, if possible, meet with an admission officer. If appropriate, set up interviews with financial aid representatives, coaches, and specific faculty members or deans.

- If the student is placed on a waiting list and wishes to keep the college as a possibility, notify the college using the return card they sent with the wait-list notification.

- Make sure the student's final transcript has been sent to the college they'll be attending.

Use the following check list as a guideline to completing a successful admissions application and campaign.

- Write or phone directly to the college to request up-to-date applications.

- Start early – don't wait until the last minute.

- Get organized – use a separate file folder for each college application.

- Be sure to read the application thoroughly and answer each question, as asked.

- Type or print each application (preferably in black ink). No longhand.

- Proofread each application. Spelling and grammatical errors are unacceptable.

- Be sure to include ONLY those extracurricular activities that are impressive to the college. They should demonstrate qualifies of leadership, duration, and activities that reinforce the student's academic and career goals mentioned in their application.

- Make copies of each completed application.

- Request the teacher recommendations early (3 weeks' preference).

- Choose teachers that best know the student.

- Provide deadlines and proper forms, including a self-addressed stamped envelope.

- Send each teacher a thank-you note, and keep each informed of the results.

- Be sure to make arrangements with the guidance department to include the student's high school transcript and distribute the applications to the colleges.

2. Résumé of Outstanding Achievement

A Résumé of Outstanding Achievement highlights the student's background and abilities. It allows for a quick review of the student's background to showcase their abilities and talents. Similar to a job résumé, the Résumé of Outstanding Achievement should quickly explain that the student:

- Is a well-rounded individual

- Has leadership capabilities

- Is organized

- Is confident and mature

- Has the capability of assuming additional responsibilities

- Has a game plan and is motivated to achieve a goal

- Has the qualities the school is look for

- DESERVES ACCEPTANCE!

3. Essays

Use the following checklist as a guideline to writing successful admission's essays.

- List the initial thoughts that the student would like to emphasize about themselves.

- Focus in on the topics that the student feels would reflect what they want to say.

- Write a tentative statement that would reflect what the student wants to say.

- Write a list of details that could be used to support their statement. The student may wish to use their <u>Résumé of Outstanding Achievement</u> as a guide.

- Arrange this list of details into a well-ordered outline.

- Demonstrate the student's intellectual curiosity, dedication, and commitment to goals, ability to complete tasks, leadership, and self-control.

- Write a first draft of the student's admission essay.

- Revise the first draft, paying special attention to the introductory and concluding paragraphs, as well as to transitions between the paragraphs.

- Proofread the revised essay at least twice: once for spelling, punctuation, usage, and other mechanical errors and a second time for meaning and overall effectiveness.

- Have someone else proofread the student's essay and make suggestions for improvement.

- Be sure the essay is within the recommended length.

- Use words and phrases that are common to the student.

- Do not overuse adjectives or adverbs.

4. Interviews

Use the following checklist for the student as a guideline for a successful admission interview.

- Practice for the interview. The student should be prepared to answer obvious questions. Consult the guidance department for these standard questions and review them with the student's counselor or parents.

- Practice makes perfect. Arrange the first interview at the college in which the student is least interested in attending.

- The student should relax and be themselves.

- Be alert and to the point. Make the interview easy for the interviewer.

- Be sure the student is neat and presentable.

- Provide the interviewer with a copy of the student's Résumé of Outstanding Achievement.

- Showcase abilities and talents. Stay positive.

- Do not dwell on a particular question. Show consideration for the interviewer's time.

- The student should not make lofty statements about themselves. Be humble.

- Avoid negatives about the student or making excuses for any sub par performance.

- Be prepared to answer the following questions:
    - Describe the ideal college
    - Which other colleges is the student considering
    - Which college is their top choice

- Send a thank-you note to each interviewer within 3 days after the interview.

Appendix C
Alternative Ways To Reduce Costs

Let's quickly examine some more innovative payment options in case you did not get enough money for your child's college education. Or, if you are the parent of a high school junior, these payment options will help you to understand where to turn if the schools let you down and you still need more money for college.

To begin with, colleges and universities are receiving less money from the federal and state governments. There is also a trend towards less FREE money and more loans being given out to help fund a college education.

Some schools, particularly the private universities, have more flexibility when it comes to negotiating for a better financial aid package, while others, like state colleges, have very little room to do anything. This means it is imperative for you, as a parent, to understand **all** of the payment options available to you just in case the college your child has their heart set on offers less than you expect or need when awarding your financial aid.

Have Your Child Start Out At A State School And Then Transfer To A Private College
If your child gets accepted to both private universities and state schools, and he/she prefers to go to one of the private schools – the first thing you need to look at is how much is it really going to cost you to send him/her to that school. If the private university offers you an excellent package, which makes it approximately the same cost to you whether you send your child to private or state, simply send your child to their top choice.

If, however, the private university offers you a less than competitive package, and sending your child there will put you deep into debt, think about sending them to a state school for two years and then have them transfer over to a private university.

You will probably end up saving yourself about $30,000, and your child will end up with a diploma from a private university. However, it is important to realize that if your son/daughter does not plan to get top grades (A- or above) at the state school, they are going to have a tough time transferring over to a top private university. Also, schools tend not to offer their best packages to transfer students, but it may balance out due to the tuition savings.

Think About Sending Your Child To A College That Offers Cooperative Education
About 900 colleges and universities across the country offer programs where students can alternate between full-time study and a full-time job. This differs from work/study in that work/study jobs tend to be jobs that students are not interested in for a couple of hours a day until they have earned the amount of the award.

On the other hand, cooperative education offers periods of full-time employment in jobs that the student is interested in pursuing after they graduate. The student usually makes enough money to pay for a good portion of tuition and they have a much better chance of landing a good job after they graduate. The only downfall is it usually takes 5 years to graduate, but it may be well worth it since in addition to the degree they hold, they also have valuable, real-world experience.

Have Your Child Take The Military Route

There are two different options. The first one is the Reserve Officer Training Corps, which has branches at many colleges. To qualify for an ROTC Scholarship, which usually covers full or partial tuition plus $100 a month allowance, your child must apply in his/her senior year of high school. They should also have good grades and 1200 (verbal and math) or above SAT scores.

The other option is applying to one of the service academies, which are extremely difficult to get into. To apply, your child must have excellent grades, SAT scores, pass a physical, and have a recommendation from a Congressman or Senator. If your child can get past all of the above, they will enjoy a FREE college education.

The only downside of going the military route is that your child will be required to serve several years in the military after they graduate.

Look Into Outside Scholarships To Help Pay For College

True, private scholarships only make up 1% of all monies available for paying for college, but you definitely will not get any of this money if you do not apply for it.

Caution – There are many scholarship search companies or Internet searches that promise you millions of dollars of unclaimed scholarships. Most of these search services are bogus and will charge you too much for their service. However, if you find an "ethical", and up-to-date search company that will run a search for you for a fair price ($50 - $100), it may be well worth it. See Appendix E.

Try Borrowing From An Innovative Loan Program

Before you look into any type of loan programs, do your best to qualify for federally subsidized loans that are interest free and principal free until your child graduates. If you still need to borrow more money, try borrowing from your 401(k) plan or a pension plan. Many plans will allow you to borrow up to 50% of the value of the plan or up to $50,000 interest free. You should also think about taking out a home equity loan instead of a commercial loan since your interest payments may be tax deductible.

Locate And Apply For Every "Need-Based" Scholarship, Grant and Low Interest Loans That Your Child May Be Eligible For

Find, or get help finding, all the "need-based" sources of funding through the federal government, the state you live in, and the colleges and universities your child is applying to (in-state or out-of-state schools). Most of these financial aid programs can be applied for by simply filling out the federal form (the FAFSA) and, in some cases, the Institutional Form (the Financial Aid Profile or CSS form).

Send Your Child To A Community College For Their First Two Years Of School

If your child works hard and gets good grades, they can usually transfer to a top private university. This way, they can get a diploma from a prestigious school for half the cost.

Choose Colleges That Have Innovative Payment Plans

Don't only pay attention to the normal college search criteria like courses offered, academic and athletic reputation, geographic location, etc. Instead, make sure you inquire about special scholarships, installment plans, guaranteed cost plans, and tuition reductions for good grades. Remember, if you don't ask – they won't tell.

Have Your Child Complete Four Years Of College In Three Years
Your child will have to attend summer school, but you will save the 7-8% increase in tuition for the fourth year.

Have Your Child Enroll In Advanced Placement Classes Or Enroll In College Level Courses While They Are Still In High School
Every college level course they place out of is money you will not have to pay when they go to college. Considering college credits can cost as much as $300 each, having your child place out of these courses can save you money.

Tuition Reductions

According to a tuition reduction executive summary released by the National Association of College and University Business Officers, the nation's private colleges continue to discount the price of acquiring an education. Many private colleges offer discounts to stay competitive with lower cost state colleges, because private colleges receive little or no support from state tax dollars.

Tuition reductions come from many private colleges' own institution funds and are given to students in the form of a merit grant and scholarship. In other words, the college will discount its "sticker price" to help attract students to its institution, regardless of the family's income level and qualifications for need-based financial aid.

Tuition reductions allow many private colleges to compete with lower cost public universities for the best students. In many cases, these discounts will lower tuition costs into the same price range as a public university. Families looking for a quality college education at a reduced cost should apply to these lesser-known private schools.

It is important for the parents to ask for information on merit grants and scholarships and other incentives at these private colleges, as they differ from college to college.

Appendix D
Major Mistakes to Avoid

Waiting Until January (Or Even Worse, After January) Of Your Child's Senior Year Of High School To Start Working On Your College Financial Aid Planning
Since financial aid is based on your previous year's income and assets, it is imperative to start your planning as soon as possible before January of your child's senior year. If you want to legally set up your income and assets so you can maximize your eligibility for financial aid, you must start working on this at least one year in advance, preferably in the beginning of your child's junior year of high school. The longer you wait and the closer it gets to your child's senior year, the tougher it gets to set up your financial picture without creating a "red flag" for the colleges and universities. It is also important for you to know what your "Expected Family Contribution" is so you can start saving for it. You should also know which schools will give you the best packages before you start visiting and applying to them.

Going Through The Financial Aid Process Or Implementing Strategies By Yourself
This allows the schools and the federal government, instead of you, to keep control over the process. People will readily use a doctor when they get sick, a lawyer when they get sued, but are reluctant to contact their CPA, financial advisor or a Certified College Planner to help them understand all of their options. College is one of your family's single biggest investments. College funding laws change each year. Your family financial situation changes each year. What if you had a trained college funding specialist and full time College Service Center with you through all 4 years? Use an expert who can help you through this process, maximize your aid, keep you informed, give you direction, answer your questions, and complete the paperwork in a timely manner is an invaluable asset in the process. Make sure you get everything you are entitled to. See Appendix F.

Getting Lulled Into A False Sense Of Security
It is never too early to begin planning for the expense of higher education. If you think that you have plenty of time before you are going to need the money, you most likely will not have enough and may not receive much, if any, financial aid. The earlier you begin planning for the entire college experience for your child; the better off you will be at making college an affordable reality.

Start Now
This is the most important point on the entire checklist. **Since the financial aid your child will be awarded is based on the current tax year, it is imperative that you start your planning now.** Failure to do so could cost you a great deal of money and lost opportunities for your child. Do not make the same mistake that most parents do, and put off this planning until another time. If you want to get the maximum amount of money from each school, you have got to set up your finances properly, fill out the forms accurately and on time, and negotiate with colleges and universities to get the best possible financial aid package. Unfortunately, guidance counselors do not have the time or the training to do these things, so you cannot rely on them to help you maximize your eligibility for college funding. College aid officers may offer to help you apply for financial aid; however, they have a limited number of funds to give out to a large number of people. Think twice before you let a guidance counselor or college aid officer "help" you apply for college funding, as it may turn out to be a very expensive mistake.

Do Not Miss Out On Annual Strategy Planning To Reduce Your Family EFC And IM
This is one of the most valuable and often missed parts of the college planning process. Most families and professionals are simply not familiar enough with the ever-changing financial aid rules. Again, let your CPA, financial advisor or a Certified College Planning Specialist assist you.

Fill Out All Your Forms Completely And Accurately
The college financial process is an annual event. FAFSA forms have to be filled out every year. The college profile is an annual event. College Stafford and Plus loans are done one year at a time. **90% of college forms are filled out incorrectly and are kicked back,** losing precious time and putting you at the back of the line in a process that is known to be on a first come basis. Be in the other 10%, at the front of the line each year, simply because your paperwork was done right the first time. Make a college-planning checklist that keeps everyone and everything on track and on time. Remember, financial aid is awarded on a first-come, first-served basis. If you submit your forms with errors or omissions, it will probably "bump" the financial aid forms and you will have to resubmit them at a later time. Also, make sure you get your forms in on time. Most schools have different deadlines and if you miss their deadline, you will almost definitely get less funding. The moral of the story is – do your forms correctly the first time!

Do Not Be Afraid To Negotiate For A Better Financial Aid Package
A school's financial aid package is not fixed in stone. Just because they offer you a certain package does not mean you have to accept it. If you know how to calculate your "expected family contribution" and you find out what the school's history of giving out financial aid is, you can usually get a pretty accurate idea of what you should have received. If the school's offer is way off, write a letter to negotiate. Don't be afraid to ask!

Be Sure To Apply For Financial Aid Even If You Do Not Think You Will Be Eligible
Most families who make between $30,000 - $100,000 per year and own a home do qualify for some forms of financial aid. Sadly, many parents are under the misconception that they won't qualify so they don't even try. This is a huge mistake since you definitely won't be offered any money if you don't apply. Even if you do not qualify based on financial "need", many schools will not consider you for "non-need" based aid if you do not apply for "need-based" aid. So regardless of what you think your eligibility to be, it is always worth a try to receive financial aid.

In Summary
The world of financial aid is one that will benefit anyone who is able to demonstrate a need for it. The most significant way to utilize the many financial aid awards out there is to first understand how you become eligible and how the amounts you are eligible for are determined. Lowering your EFC by actively positioning assets and money is the most secure way not only to make college an affordable reality, but also to give you the ability to continue building your retirement. Every school has aid that is allotted and available to those who need or deserve it. By taking the right measures and implementing the proper strategies, you and your child may demonstrate need no matter what your income level. Your student must also play a vital role by setting himself or herself apart from the crowd in order to get the schools' attention. When your student is desirable, the schools will make offers in order to get your student on their campuses. When properly

planned for and understood, the financial aid process is a powerful ally when it comes time to save and pay for college.

APPENDIX E
SCHOLARSHIP SEARCHES

"There are scholarship and grant monies that go unused each year because people don't know how to access them." That is what the computerized scholarship search companies claim. It is NOT TRUE. The colleges themselves control most of the available college scholarships and grants, and only 1% of them are available through outside sources. The following sections will help parents identify the deceptive scholarship search offers, conduct their own LOCAL scholarship search and introduce a low cost computerized search used by colleges and libraries around the country.

What The Parents Should Do

1. Learn how to identify the common traits of deceptive, computerized scholarship search offers and how they prey on desperate parents by using misleading wording in their sales pitch.

2. Conduct a scholarship search from local organizations such as the Chamber of Commerce, Rotary Club, churches, etc. These local private scholarships and grants are more accessible to the student.

3. Review nationwide scholarship searches from the companies used by colleges and libraries around the country. The financial advisor may wish to use these services if he believes that "time is money" and he wants to save hours of research conducting a scholarship search specific to a particular student.

Recognizing The Deceptive Scholarship Search

Factors that are typical of deceptive scholarship search offers are:

- Costs range from $79 to $299.

- Page after page of out-of-date lists of private scholarships and grants are received. Most do not fit the student's profile. The student must do all the legwork, including applications and compliance with the terms and conditions of the scholarship.

- Promises a "rock-solid" guarantee.

- Any guarantee requires proof of rejection from the entire potential list of sources. NO credible foundation will notify the numerous rejections.

- Frequently states that they have confirmed the student's "eligibility" in an award. They don't know the student.

- A notice of this great possibility will be frequently received with a note or postcard.

Local Scholarships are the Best Choice

Scholarships and grants from local organizations are more likely to fit a student's profile, and the odds of success increase dramatically by applying for these private sector monies. These local private scholarships and grants are more accessible. The student's high school guidance counselor will generally be aware of local scholarships and can help the student identify those that match the student's qualifications. Also, the family should check for scholarship offerings by the various membership and product relationships used by the family. For example, if the family is a member of any fraternal insurance organizations, those entities will often offer scholarships to members or to children of members. Similarly, the family's household insurance provider, local utility company, or similar entities may offer scholarships to customers.

Here are some of the places the student can begin to look for scholarship funds:

1. High School Guidance Department

2. Parent/Teacher's Association

3. Chamber of Commerce

4. Local Libraries

5. Local Community/Technical College(s)

6. Yellow Pages (under Foundations)

7. Churches

8. Clubs

9. Unions

10. Trade Associations

11. Fraternal Organizations

12. American Legion Posts

13. Businesses (Human Relations Department)

14. Local Pageants

A National Database Of Scholarships and Grants

Even though the private sector produces only 1% of the available college financial aid, many families still wish to pursue every possible source of monies to reduce their college costs. Here are the common traits of a respectable computerized scholarship search:

1. *Low cost.* The local library may have a FREE scholarship database. If the cost of a customized database search is high, it is probably worth the time and effort for the student to complete his own database research.

2. *No guarantee.* In this highly competitive field of private sector scholarships and grants, there is NEVER a guarantee the student will actually win monies. Therefore a credible company will never offer a guarantee. Their only guarantee is that the student will save time using their predetermined, verified database.

3. *Annually verified list of sources.* Every foundation or company that offers a scholarship or grant or endowment usually operates their program under a non-

profit status and must register each year with the Internal Revenue Service. A credible search company will verify the continuing status of each source every year.

4. *Credibility.* If the database used by the search company is also sold to libraries and colleges, the financial advisor is most likely tapping into a credible source.

Legitimate Scholarship Searches

Most of these private monies available to students are from local organizations and companies. Very few nationwide awards fit a particular student; however, even these can be accessed free of charge from computer programs at local colleges and libraries. The following are free online scholarship search databases:

- FastWeb
  www.fastweb.com

- MACH24
  www.collegenet.com

- SRN Express
  www.rams.com/srn

- MOLIS (Minority Online Info)
  www.lights.com/hytelnet/oth/oth023.html

NOTE: *FastWeb creates a private mailbox that updates and notifies by message any new awards that match the student's special criteria.*

Scholarship Application Tips

Once the advisor locates awards that best fit the profile of the student, complete the applications. Keep in mind that each application has a specific deadline. Here are some tips to guide the student in completing the private scholarship applications:

TIP #1: Pay Attention To Deadlines

Have the application arrive several days prior to the due date. Always send applications with a "merchandise receipt" to make sure they get there. Note: There is a difference between "merchandise" and "certified" receipts. With a merchandise receipt, anyone can sign for the application. Only the addressee can sign for the application on a certified receipt. Thus, if the addressee does not pick up the mail, the application may not make the deadline.

TIP #2: Start the Application With A "Thank You" Cover Letter

A sample cover letter is shown on the following page.

"Sample Packet Cover Letter"

August 1, 2004

Mary Smith, President
XXX Scholarship Committee
Orlando Central Parkway
Orlando, FL   XXXXX

Dear Ms. Smith:

This letter is an introduction of myself, (your name), and my desire to participate in the (xxx) Scholarship Program. I have been accepted to (Name of College) for the 2004 fall term.

I would like to thank you and the (xxx) Scholarship Committee for supporting college bound students with an opportunity for financial assistance through your scholarship program. Enclosed you will find my application form, high school transcript, ACT results, letters of recommendation, and other pertinent information per your requirements.

Again, thank you for your interest on my behalf and for the youth of our state.

Respectfully,

(Your name)

Enclosures

<u>Tip #3</u>: **Answer Their "Request"**
While this seems obvious, one must construct the application to make it EASY for the committee to see that the student has provided everything that was required. Provide the items in the order that they are listed in the application. If possible, do not mix items on the same page.

<u>Tip #4</u>: **Add Extra Items To Your Application (If Not Prohibited)**
This is where a student gets to be creative to find ways and things that present the student in a positive light to the selection committee. Here are a few ideas to get started:

1. Write a short essay on "MY EDUCATION/CAREER GOALS." Try to keep to one page but no more than two. Write a paragraph or two on how this scholarship award would help the student reach the Education/Career Goals.

2. Include any letter from the guidance counselor congratulating the student on being in the top 10% of the class, as this will put the student in a "positive light" and show that hard work is recognized.

3. One of the best extra items is a letter of acceptance for admission to "any" college. A letter of acceptance shows that the student is serious, but it does not "lock" the student into using the award at that college.

If the scholarship application is not for a specific college, the student can use the award at any college. The student does not have to use it at the college used in the application. The student can notify the scholarship award committee of where to send the award.

Find things that make the student look good and share them with the committee. Limit extras to three or four at the most. Too many extras may "sour" an application. Again, make sure the student is <u>not forbidden</u> to add extra items before doing so.

<u>Tip #5</u>: **Personalized Letter(s) Of Recommendation**
A letter of recommendation conveys that the student took the time to make the application special. When the student has a letter of recommendation addressed to the specific organization or person that is administering the application process, it says that the student took the time and effort to make this letter "special" for them.

Offer to do much of the work for the writer of the letter of recommendation. If the student wants to apply to twenty scholarship programs, ask if the student can put the application on the computer so the TO ADDRESSEE can be personalized for each application and the writer only has to sign their name twenty times. If the writer has personalized letterhead, ask for blank copies to be used in this process.

Use this letter of recommendation as an "EXTRA ITEM" if the application does not specifically require a letter of recommendation. Try to obtain three to five letters of recommendation. This will let the student pick and choose which one or ones to send in for a specific application. Never send more than three for an application unless the directions ask for more.

Tip #6: Proofread All Materials And Neatness Is A MUST
Use correct grammar and spelling. If the student has a problem in this area, ask an English teacher to help with proofreading the essay, cover letter, extra items included, and even letters of recommendation prepared by others. When there are hundreds of applications to review, correctness and neatness becomes the first screen out factor. Only when the "pile" is smaller does the content of the application start to become a factor in the selection process.

Tip #7: Submit Your Application In A Clear Plastic Folder
Now that the application is complete, the final presentation tip is to place all of the items in a clear plastic folder with a slide locking binder. Use the inexpensive clear binders and include the "Thank You Cover Letter" on top. Include a wallet size picture of the student in the lower left side of the packet. The next items in the application packet are those required in the application. Next, add any extra items (if not forbidden) and finally, include any letter(s) of recommendation.

Finally, the application packet should represent a great looking presentation. Do not ruin the appearance by folding it to fit a small envelope. Use a 9 x 12 (or larger if necessary) so the application arrives looking great. Remember to send it merchandise receipt.

Tip #8: Find Something That Interests The Student And Do Some Volunteer Work
There are many local community service awards available to students, some of which do not involve a great deal of work. There have been fairly large community service scholarships awarded to people with just 20 hours of service. The key is to find an area the student likes and have them get involved.

Finding community service isn't difficult. Walk into any senior care home. Tell them the student wants to volunteer 2 hours per week. The student will get to talk to some very appreciative and lonely people. In just 10 weeks, the student will have donated 20 hours and the volunteer coordinator at that home would probably write a great reference.

Summary of Scholarship Searches
There is scholarship money available from private sources for both affluent and non-affluent clients. The student's best chance of obtaining private scholarships is to apply for scholarships given by local sources. The client should be made aware of the traits of "scholarship search scams".

APPENDIX F
INFORMATION ON THE INTERNET

On-Line Databases

College Funding, Inc.
www.solutionsforcollege.com

Peterson's CollegeQuest Search
www.collegequest.com

College Board Search
www.collegeboard.org

FishNet: The College Guide
www.mycollegeguide.org/ACG/search.html

Studyabroad.com
www.studyabroad.com

All About College
www.allaboutcollege.com

Community College Web
www.mcli.dist.maricopa.edu/cc

Professional and Graduate Schools
www.gradschools.com/search.html

Selecting Schools

CampusTours.com
www.campustours.com

Considering College Quality
www.petersons.com/ugrad/consider.html

Getting Ready for University
www.campusaccess.com

Distance Education

Distance Education and Training Council
www.detc.org

Online Education
www.caso.com

Globewide Network Academy
www.gnacademy.org

Yahoo!
www.yahoo.com/education

Standardized Tests

Educational Testing Service (ETS)
www.ets.org

The Wordsmyth S.A.T. Dictionary
www.eduprep.com/wwmain.sat.html

College Power Prep
www.powerprep.com

Applications On-Line

CollegeNet's ApplyWeb Online Application
www.applyweb.com

XAP Applications
www.xap.com

Undergraduate Admission E-Apps
www.eapp.com/univ/uglist/htm

Princeton Review's Apply!
www.weapply.com

APPENDIX G
Why CPAs, Financial Advisors, & Certified College Planning Specialists (CCPS) Are Necessary

Appendix of Strategies

The following is a reference guide of education cost-cutting strategies for families of all income levels. These seldom-used strategies were created by some of the top minds in educational funding and can provide families with financial opportunities to help fund their tuition costs. They can also be found in the corresponding sections earlier in this book. They include:

- Tax Strategies

- Financial Planning Strategies

- Financial Aid Strategies

- Household Strategies

- Academic Strategies

- Creative Borrowing Strategies

- Other College Cost Cutting Strategies

Asset Strategies For Financial Aid Families

1. The family should inquire about the college's policy concerning annuities and the cash value of life insurance before considering the purchase of these investments. Some private colleges, usually the more elite ones, will assess these assets.

2. If the child has earned income, they may consider saving for college by purchasing a Roth IRA.

3. Since retirement accounts will not be assessed in the Expected Family Contribution (EFC) formulas, saving for college using retirement accounts and then borrowing against the accounts to pay for college may be a viable strategy.

4. If the family plans a purchase in the near future, in may be wise to use an assessable asset, such as cash, to purchase a non-assessable personal asset, such as a personal computer.

5. Personal debt cannot be used to reduce the net worth of an assessable asset. However, personal items, such as cars, boats, motorcycles or jewelry, are not considered assets in the financial aid formula.

6. The family should consider paying down personal debt with an assessable asset (savings).

7. Claiming a second home interest expense deduction on Schedule A for a boat or motor home makes these assessable assets.

8. Since the Federal Methodology (FM) formula does not assess family farm assets, the family may consider using non-farm assessable assets, such as CDs, to pay down farm-related debt.

9. The family may want to delay signing the financial aid applications until after the older parent's birthday. Under the FM formula this will increase the "Asset Protection Allowance".

10. If the family has assets subject to a life estate, the family should appeal to the Financial Aid Administrator (FAA) because these assets cannot be liquidated to pay for college costs.

11. If the family has assets tied up in probate, the family should appeal to the FAA if there will be no distribution of assets during college years.

12. The family can reduce the value of a trust by spending the trust assets for the benefit of the student (e.g., trust buys a car for college or pays for the student's private high school tuition). If the family takes assets out of a trust or custodial account and the assets are not used for the benefit of the student, there can be some adverse legal and tax consequences.

13. If the family's child's access to trust funds is restricted until after college years, the value of the trust should be appealed to the FAA.

14. If the family's child is the beneficiary of a Qualified Tuition Plan (QTP) and qualifies for financial aid, the family should consider rolling the QTP to another beneficiary.

15. If the family qualifies for the "Simplified EFC" exception, neither the family's assets nor those of the student will be assessed in the FM formula.

16. If the family qualifies for the "Zero EFC" exception, the student will automatically have a zero EFC.

17. The Institutional Methodology formula will also assess the student's siblings' assets, at the parents' assessment rate.

18. At what date would the value of the assets be the least? If possible, the financial aid application form should be signed at the date the assets are at their lowest value.

19. Can the family shift income-generating assets to growth assets during college years? The growth asset is still assessed but no income is generated.

Asset Strategies For Upper Income Families

1. Funding a life insurance policy over a period of several years could be a viable option. It can allow the family to take maximum advantage of tax-deferred growth and tax advantaged withdrawals for college, as well as retirement.

2. Gifts that families pay directly to an educational institution (either elementary and high school or college) for their child's tuition will not reduce the annual $12,000 gift tax exclusion for that child. The gifts must be made directly to the educational institution.

3. If families wanted to transfer more funds to their child or grandchild than the annual $12,000 gift exclusion, they could accomplish this by making a loan to the child for the amount in excess of the $12,000 gift exclusion limit. They would then forgive up to $12,000 per year until the loan balance is zero.

4. There is a special rule for contributions to a QTP that exceed the annual gift tax exclusion. If a contribution in excess of the annual $12,000 gift tax exclusion is made in one year, the family may elect to have the contribution treated as if made over five years.

5. Charitable remainder trusts can produce a double tax savings that can be used to help fund college costs. In a typical charitable remainder trust, you would donate a remainder interest in an asset to a charity. The family would receive a current charitable donation tax deduction, remove the asset from their estate, and retain an income interest in the asset to help fund college costs.

6. A highly appreciated low-yielding asset can be contributed to a charitable remainder trust.

7. Since the charitable remainder trust is exempt from taxation, the asset can be sold tax-free. The proceeds can then be reinvested in a higher-yielding investment without depleting the investment principal.

8. The Roth IRA is an attractive vehicle to use for college, because of the tax and penalty-free withdrawal of original contributions.

9. A grandparent can will their Roth IRA to a grandchild. The minimum distribution rules will require distributions from the Roth IRA to be based on the life expectancy of the grandchild. The grandchild could take minimum distributions (the balance of the account continues to grow tax-free) until college years and then withdraw additional tax-free funds for college.

10. The Voluntary Employees' Beneficiary Association (VEBA) can allow for large, flexible, and fully tax-deductible contributions. The assets will accumulate and compound on a tax-deferred basis while remaining protected from both personal and corporate creditors.

11. If additional funds for college are needed, the family should consider a Federal Parent's Loan for Undergraduate Students (PLUS loan). A PLUS loan is a signature loan with an interest rate capped at 9%. These loans can be made only for undergraduate college expenses.

12. If additional funds for college are needed, the family should consider having their child obtain an unsubsidized Stafford loan. Since an unsubsidized Stafford loan is in the child's name, the child can deduct the student loan interest expense. Also, if the family cannot deduct student loan interest expense (because of the income limitations), an unsubsidized Stafford loan in the student's name is preferable to a PLUS loan in the parent's name.

13. If additional funds for college are needed, the family should consider having their child obtain a Sallie Mae signature student loan. A Sallie Mae signature student loan is in the child's name and therefore, they can deduct the student loan interest expense. Because of the deductible interest expense, these loans may be preferable to a PLUS loan in the parent's name.

14. The family can either use an equity line of credit or a second mortgage on their residence for college funds. The interest paid can be deducted as an itemized deduction.

15. The family can borrow, up to a certain amount, from their retirement account, if the account allows borrowing. Usually the interest rate and repayment terms are favorable. However, if the family member loses their job, the outstanding loan balance may have to be immediately repaid or taxable income will occur. Also, if the loans are not repaid within a certain time period, usually five years, the outstanding principal balance will become taxable.

16. The family could loan money to their child for college. The family would receive payments on the loan from their child. The difference between the rate of return the family is receiving on the money loaned to their child and the interest rate their child would have paid from an outside source could be used to reduce the family's cost of college.

17. The deduction for alimony creates an opportunity to shift income from a higher to a lower tax bracket spouse. Additional payments that can be considered alimony are medical insurance and other expenditures, such as mortgage payments, real estate taxes, insurance, utilities, life insurance premiums, and college expenses, made on behalf of a former spouse under a divorce decree or separation agreement.

18. Under the financial aid rules for divorce or separation situations, the income and assets of only the custodial parent are used to compute a child's eligibility for financial aid. (Note: Some private colleges will also factor in the income and assets of the non-custodial parent.) Therefore, the family should carefully consider with whom their child will live during the college years.

19. The family can use a 401(k) wraparound plan to put excess 401(k) contributions into a non-qualified plan. These excess contributions can be used to fund a child's future college costs. The family does not have to report taxable income before the excess contributions are put into the non-qualified plan. The family must make two separate elections: (1) to contribute to the 401(k) plan and, (2) to have the excess contributions transferred to the non-qualified plan.

Income Strategies For Financial Aid Families

1. Since loans proceeds are not assessed, it may be better to borrow funds during college years rather than attempting to pay for college by striving to increase earnings, which will decrease financial aid eligibility.

2. The student should avoid cash gifts from people other than parents during college yeas, as these are treated as "untaxed income" in the financial aid system. If cash gifts are going to be given to the student, they should be given in non-college years. Alternatively, loans could be given to the student during college years and then a cash gift could be given to repay the loan(s) after college years.

3. Cash gifts, which are paid directly to the college for tuition and fees (from people other than the parents), should be avoided. These gifts will be treated as a student "resource" and a dollar-for-dollar deduction in financial aid.

4. Since the current year's contribution to a retirement plan will be assessed as "untaxed income", the family should maximize contributions to a retirement plan during non-college years and minimize contributions during college years.

5. Parents should avoid withdrawals from retirement, pension, annuity, or life insurance plans during college years because both the interest, included in the Adjusted Gross Income (AGI), and the principal withdrawal, included as "untaxed income", will be assessed. If withdrawals of assessable assets are made, an assessment of this withdrawal should be appealed to the FAA. The appeal should be based on the fact that the transfer of principal from one type of asset to another type of asset does not create an additional source of funds to pay for college.

6. If a taxable conversion from a regular IRA to a Roth IRA is made, the assessment of this taxable rollover income should be appealed to the FAA. Remember that non-taxable rollovers are not assessed.

7. Eligibility for the Employment Expense Allowance deduction is allowed only if both parents have earned income. This could be accomplished by hiring a non-working spouse in the family business.

8. The family should consider having the family's business establish a medical reimbursement plan (IRC Sec.105) for an employee-spouse in order to shift medical expenses from Schedule A to the business schedule and, consequently, lower the family's AGI.

9. The student's income should be kept at approximately $3,000 during college years. Shifting income to the student should be considered if the student does not have this much income. This will lower the parents' AGI without having a negative effect on the student's financial aid eligibility.

10. Wages from closely held entities should be kept down during college years.

11. Minimize the amount of state or local tax refunds during college years. To insure that refunds are not received, accurate withholding or estimate payments should be made.

12. Consider accelerating or postponing capital asset purchases during college years in order to lower business income through depreciation or Additional First Year Depreciation (AFYD) on the capital asset.
13. The family should consider accelerating tax-deductible expenses during college years.

14. The family should consider obtaining commercial bank loans rather than taxable Commodity Credit Corporation (CCC) loans (farmers) during college years.

15. The family should consider selling stocks in non-college years that would generate capital gain distributions during college years.

16. Avoid income distributions from estates or trusts during college years.

17. The family should consider not itemizing tax deductions during college years.

Income Strategies For Upper Income Families
Outright gifts of appreciated assets to the child or grandchild may be an effective way to shift income and assets to the child or grandchild. Significant income and estate tax savings can be achieved by outright gifts. However, control of assets that are gifted outright to the child or grandchild will be lost immediately.

1. When a family's income reaches a certain level, all or part of their personal exemptions is phased out. Therefore, they would not receive any tax benefit from their child's personal exemption. However, if the child can show that they, and not the family, are providing over half of their support, they can claim the personal exemption on their tax return.

2. Since the family is in at least the 28% tax bracket, they should consider gifting appreciated assets to their child (over age 18) and then have the child sell the asset. If the child is in the 15% tax bracket, his capital gains rate would be at 5%, as opposed to the family's 15% capital gains rate.

3. Families can receive tax benefits if they employ their child. Since the child will receive "earned" income, he will not be subject to the "Kiddie Tax", even if he is less than 18 years of age. Also, because it is earned income, the child will be able to utilize his standard deduction. Another benefit of a child having earned income is that he can contribute to a Roth or regular IRA for future college costs.

4. A family can hire their spouse in their business and establish a medical reimbursement plan for the spouse and the rest of their family. In effect, this would make non-deductible medical expenses deductible business expenses.

5. A family limited partnership can provide the family with a way to shift income to their children and reduce their estate. Typically, in a family limited partnership, the family will be the general partner and their children will be limited partners. The limited partners cannot make investment, business, or management decisions. The family would make annual gifts of partnership interests to their children.

6. A family may gift the maximum amount allowed by the annual gift tax exclusion ($12,000) and take a note from their child for the balance of the funds needed for college. Then, instead of the child having to make payments on the note, the parent could forgive a portion of the principal (and interest) each year equal to the annual gift tax exclusion.

7. A qualified tuition program (QTP) can be used to shift income to a child or grandchild. The income generated from assets gifted to a QTP grows tax-deferred. When the child receives distributions from the QTP for college, the accumulated income is taxed to him.

8. Tax shelters are a form of deferring income. One of the best tax shelters for college is an oil and gas investment. As a general rule, the tax write-off on an oil and gas investment will not exceed 100% of the amount of the investment. Working interests in oil and gas ventures are generally not treated as passive activities.

9. Since the tax applies to unearned income of a child under eighteen years of age, one strategy to avoid the Kiddie Tax is to invest the child's assets in investments, such as municipal bonds or growth stocks, that generate tax-exempt or tax-deferred income until the child reaches age eighteen.

10. A parent can elect to have the interest on their child's U.S. EE savings bonds taxed each year and, if the child is not subject to the Kiddie Tax, the interest will be taxed at this lower tax rate. Therefore, the year that a child redeems the bonds, they will not have to pay any tax on the proceeds.

11. A family's business can establish a fringe benefit program for their child/employee. If the type of fringe benefit established by the business is tax deductible and taxable to a child/employee (e.g., employer provided automobile), this will cause an income-shifting effect. If the type of fringe benefit established by the business is deductible by a business but not taxable to a child/employee (e.g., medical reimbursement), the tax savings can be used to cut the cost of college.

Household Strategies For Financial Aid Families

1. The financial aid application should be signed on the date when the household status is the most beneficial.

2. If the student's parents are divorced, the income and assets of the parent with whom the student lived the most in the twelve months must be reported. Therefore, the income and assets of the parent with whom the student lives with during college years must be considered.

3. If the student's parents are divorced and the student lived equally with the parents (e.g., joint custody), the income and assets of the parent who provided the most support in the last twelve months must be reported. Therefore, the income and assets of the parent with whom the student lives with during college years must be considered.

4. When structuring a divorce agreement, it may be better to give the custodial parent more assets and less income.

5. If the student has a stepparent, the income and assets of the stepparent must be reported. Therefore, the timing of the signing of the financial aid application and the marriage of the parent/step-parent should be considered.

6. In order to list a child who is not living with the parent as a member of the household, the parent should provide over half the support of that child.

7. If the child does not meet one of the criteria to be automatically considered an "independent student", but is financially independent of the parent and does not live with the parent, the student can appeal to the FAA for "independent student" status.

Education Tax Incentive Strategies For All Families
1. If the parents' AGI is too high to claim the Hope Credit (HC) or Lifetime Learning Credit (LC) the parents should consider giving up the exemption for the student so that the student can claim the HC or LC. The student cannot claim the exemption unless they are providing over half of their support.

2. The timing of the payment of qualified expenses may ensure that the maximum HC or LC can be claimed.

3. If a college does not have a set payment ordering system for tax-free grants and scholarships, the parent can arrange the payments to non-tuition and fee expenses in order to be eligible for the HC or LC. (This will cause all or a portion of the scholarship to be taxable.)

4. Withdrawals from the Coverdell Education Savings Account (CESA) during years in which the parents are eligible for the HC or LC should be coordinated so the HC/LC can be maximized. If withdrawals from a CESA are elected to be taxable, the CESA withdrawal will not reduce qualified expenses for HC/LC.

5. A family with two students in college at the same time could consider giving up the exemption for one of the students so that one student can claim the LC and the parents could claim the LC for the other student. Thus, the family could claim two LCs.

6. The HC or LC can be claimed by the taxpayer that claims the student as a dependent, even if the college expenses are actually paid by the student or by a third party.

7. Parents whose AGI is too high to make a contribution to a CESA can make a gift to other persons and then they can make the contribution.

8. QTPs can be an effective method of shifting income to a lower tax bracket.

9. QTPs can be used as a vehicle to defer income.

10. In certain states, QTPs may be exempt from state taxation.

11. In certain states, QTP contributions may be deductible for state income tax purposes.

12. QTPs can be used to reduce estates without giving up control of the asset. The owner of the account can withdraw the account funds, subject to income taxes and penalty. A five-year averaging of the gift is allowed.

13. QTP accounts can be rolled over to another beneficiary if the current beneficiary will be eligible for financial aid.

14. The parents need to consider the financial aid impact of QTPs when deciding whether to purchase them and what type to purchase (i.e., prepaid versus college savings).

15. Interest paid on loans from relatives does not qualify for the student loan interest deduction.

16. If the parents' AGI is too high to claim a student loan interest deduction, the student could take a Federal Unsubsidized Stafford Loan or a private loan in the student's name and deduct the interest.

17. The timing of repayment of student loans to increase the student loan interest deduction should be considered.

18. Parents who are ineligible for the student loan interest deduction may consider taking out a deductible home mortgage loan.

19. If withdrawals from regular or Roth IRAs are needed to pay for college, the withdrawal should be timed to occur during college years in order to escape the 10% early withdrawal penalty.

Investment Strategies For All Families
1. U.S. Series EE bonds are tax-deferred or tax-free (when used to pay qualified education expenses), low-risk investments that can be used as part of the long-term college financial aid plan.

2. Zero coupon bonds are tax-deferred investments that lock in the current rate of interest and a specific amount on maturity. They can be used as part of the long-term college financial plan.

3. Municipal bonds are tax-free, low-risk investments that lock in the interest rate. They can be used as part of the long-term college financial plan.

4. Mutual funds are growth oriented long-term investments that allow for the switching of investments without capital gain income being realized until the investments are sold. They can be used as part of the long-term college financial plan.

5. QTPs are tax-deferred trust accounts that are used to pay for tuition, fees, and room and board at the colleges specified in the investment contract. The gifts to

these accounts can be spread over five years, which allows for large one-time gifts to these programs. Since the owner of the account can switch beneficiaries, the owner can maintain some control over the funds.

6. A Roth IRA is a long-term investment that grows tax-deferred. The withdrawals made from these accounts after age 59½ are tax and penalty-free. The non-deductible original contributions may be withdrawn tax-free for any use. In addition, there will be no 10% early withdrawal penalty on withdrawals made before age 59 ½ that are used to pay qualified college expenses.

7. IRAs are tax-deferred long-term investments. They can be withdrawn penalty-free (10% penalty for withdrawal before age 59½) to pay qualified college expenses. The contributions to these accounts are tax deductible.

8. Real estate is a long-term growth-oriented investment whose appreciation in value grows tax-deferred and will be taxed at the favorable capital gains rate when sold. If the real estate is rented, it may generate significant tax losses (through depreciation).

Academic Strategies For All Families
1. The student should try to increase their SAT/ACT test scores through study and preparatory courses.

2. The student should take as many honors or advanced courses as possible.

3. Parents should encourage the student to study. Good grades will result in grants and scholarships for the child.

4. The student should be encouraged to participate in extra-curricular activities. These activities will increase the student's chances of obtaining scholarships.

5. The student should investigate the College Level Examination Program (CLEP) at prospective colleges.

6. The student should take as many Advanced Placement (AP) courses as possible.

Admission Strategies For All Families
1. The student should apply to at least six to eight colleges. This will give the student some financial options.

2. Some colleges will waive the admission fee if requested to do so, especially in the case where the fee is a hardship.

3. Some colleges waive the admission fee if the admission application is filed over the Internet.

4. The student should apply early to attract college scholarships that are not based on the financial need of the student, but on the college's desire to meet their enrollment quota at an early date.

5. The student should not apply "early decision" unless they are on the borderline of being admitted and the desire to be admitted is greater than the need for financial aid. "Early decision" often leads to poor offers of financial aid.

6. There are some students, such as athletes, minorities, or musicians who receive special consideration for admissions approval. The family should check with the college for the types of students that receive this special consideration.

7. A college considers the quality of the admissions package - this includes the resume' of outstanding achievement, the essay, and the interview – in its decision to admit a student. The student must know these admission strategies to have an impressive admissions package.

Award Letter Strategies For All Families

1. Check the deadline date for acceptance of the award letter.

2. Check the EFC on the award letter (if it is shown) with the EFC shown on the Student Aid Report (SAR) in order to check the accuracy of EFC shown on the award letter.

3. Make sure the "true Cost of Attendance (COA)" is indicated on the award letter. If the cost of attendance is not shown or it appears to leave out some costs, determine the "true COA". Ask for the PLUS loan eligibility and then add that to your financial aid award to compute the "true COA".

4. Federal PLUS loans or Unsubsidized Stafford Loans should not be considered as financial aid; however, they both have very favorable interest rates and the interest could be tax deductible.

5. Determine if the grant and scholarship aid is renewable and what the criteria is for renewal.

6. If a college has an acceptance deadline that cannot be met, the family should ask for an extension of time, and if the college will not grant an extension of time, the family should accept the award letter. This will safeguard the award. Accepting an award letter does not commit the student to attending the college.

7. Accepting an award letter does not prevent the family from filing a future appeal of the award letter.

8. When all the award letters have been received, the family or a financial advisor should compare them to determine the best award.

9. If the award letter does not meet the expectations of the family, it should be appealed to the FAA.

10. Determine how "private scholarships" are handled. Do they reduce grants or loans in the award letter?

11. If the student has a "private scholarship", determine how it will affect a 4-year scholarship awarded by the college.

Appeal Strategies For All Families

1. If a college's FAA does not meet a family's expectations, either in the amount of the offer or in the type of aid offered (gift-aid versus self-help aid), the family should appeal to the FAA. Do not ask to "negotiate" with the FAA; the word "negotiate" offends some FAAs. Ask to "appeal" an award offer.

2. The FAA has the authority to change the information reported on the financial aid applications in any way that the FAA thinks will more clearly reflect a family's ability to pay for college. This authority is called "professional judgment".

3. The family must have specific reasons why they need more financial aid. These reasons are known as "special circumstances". The "special circumstances" should be adequately documented to make it easy for the FAA to say "yes" to the appeal.

4. Special circumstances may include:

   - Death
   - Divorce/separation
   - Disability or injury
   - Unemployment
   - Sickness, medical, or handicap expense
   - Tuition for private schools
   - Natural disasters
   - Dislocated worker
   - Unusually high child-care expenses
   - Un-reimbursed expenses shown on Form 2106
   - One-time bonus
   - Unusually high income
   - Unusually low expenses
   - Anything that can be used to convince the FAA that the child has a special need for money.

5. An appeal should request a specific amount of increased financial aid.

6. In most cases, a FAA will consider an appeal only if a financial aid application or Student Aid Report has been filed or received by the FAA.

7. An appeal can be based on the following college's interests:

   - Reward a good student who is in the upper 25% of the incoming freshman class. The freshman class profile can be obtained from the college or from Peterson's Guide to Colleges.

- The college admission officer, a coach (at NCAA Division III colleges), or department head can be enlisted to help with the appeal.

- Apply to at least six colleges. This will create competition for the student. To create competition, the student should include the following types of schools in the list of colleges that they wish to attend: (1) an in-state public, (2) a private college that is known to give good award offers, (3) a college in the same athletic conference, and (4) a comparable college that is out of the student's region of residency (colleges encourage cultural diversity in their enrollments).

- If a student receives a good award offer from a competing college, the student should ask the college of choice to "match" the other college's award offer. However, never use the word "match" in the correspondence or conversation with the FAA. The word "match" may offend some FAAs.

- Colleges with declining enrollments may be more willing to negotiate with a student because of their desire to fill empty seats.

- Colleges may have scholarships for upper-middle class and affluent families to attract good students and future benefactors.

- Colleges may have special scholarships for minority students. A student should inquire at the college for these scholarships.

- Colleges may have special scholarships for students of alumni or legacy students. A student should inquire at the college for these scholarships.

- A college's desire for cultural diversity in its enrollment may lead to increased financial aid offers for students who are from out of the college's geographic region, or who are culturally different from its "typical" student.

8. The greater the merit of the student, the better the chance of an appeal being granted by the FAA.

9. Private colleges are much more likely to grant an appeal than a public university.

10. Check the size of the college's endowment fund to see if they can afford to give more financial aid.

11. If possible, make the appeal in person or, at least, make a phone call to the FAA. Always give the personal touch, if possible.

Cost-Cutting Strategies For All Families
1. The Internet has several sites that offer discounts to students for books, travel, etc.

2. The student can participate in a three-year degree program that allows them to complete a bachelors degree in three years, while pursuing a master's or doctorate.
3. The student can attend a college with a guaranteed four-year degree program. (Guarantees graduation in four years.)

4. Some colleges offer programs that allow the student to attend five years of college for the cost of four years.

5. Some colleges offer programs that combine undergraduate with graduate studies in one degree.

6. Some colleges offer a guaranteed tuition price for four years.

7. Some colleges offer financing programs that help families spread out tuition payments.

8. Some colleges offer tuition reduction plans that are excluded from gross income, if used for undergraduate courses.

9. The student can attend a community or junior college and obtain a college degree without a high cost.

10. The student can attend a low cost community (junior) college for one or two years and then transfer to a private college and earn a degree from the prestigious private college.

11. The student can reduce costs by taking Advanced Placement (AP) courses in high school and earn college credit, which will reduce the time spent in college.

12. If the student is attending an out-of-state college, establish residency in that state in order to pay in-state tuition.

13. A low-cost alternative to be considered is Canadian schools.

14. Distance learning (DL) can be used to earn college credits.

Dictionary of Terms

ACT: American College Test

AFYD: Additional First Year Depreciation

AGI: Adjusted Gross Income

AP: Advanced Placement

CESA: Coverdell Education Savings Account. A trust account funded by non-deductible contributions used to pay for future qualified education expenses of the beneficiary of the account.

CLEP: College Level Examination Program

CCC: Commodity Credit Corporation

CCPS: Certified College Planning Specialist

COA: Cost of Attendance

DE: Distance Education (also known as Distance Learning)

DL: Distance Learning (also known as Distance Education)

EFC: Expected Family Contribution

F/\\: Financial Aid Administrator

FAFSA: Free Application for Federal Student Aid is the form that must be filed by a family to qualify for federal financial aid.

Federal Perkins Loan: Low interest, need-based loans up to $4,000; the interest rate is subsidized by the federal government until 6 months after the student leaves collage and fixed at 5%.

FM: Federal Methodology Formula; a federal formula used to calculate the Estimated Family Contribution.

HC: Hope Scholarship Credit (a non-refundable credit against an individual's federal income tax liability.

IM: Institutional Methodology Formula; an alternative formula used by some private colleges to calculate an Institution Estimated Family Contribution.

Kiddie Tax Years: Birth through age 17.

Kiddie Tax: Investment income such as interest, dividends or rental income of a child under age 18 that exceeds $1,700.

LLC or LC: Lifetime Learning Credit

MSA: Medical Savings Account

QTP: Qualified Tuition Plans, commonly called 529 Plans.

SAT: Scholastic Aptitude Test

Stafford Loans: Federal subsidized Stafford Loans are variable rate, need-based loans; the interest is paid or subsidized by the federal government until 6 months after the student leaves college; the interest rate is capped at 8.25%.

VEBA: Voluntary Employees' Beneficiary Association

PLUS Loan: Parents' Loan for Undergraduate Student. A signature loan with an interest rate capped at 9%.

UGMA: Uniform Gift to Minors

UTMA: Uniform Transfer to Minors

VUL: Variable Universal Life

WGPA: Weighted Grade Point Average

120 W. Main St., Suite 405, Van Wert, Ohio 45891   Ph. (800) 306-6340

www.CSILLC.org

Subjects covered:

- **Financial Aid Defined**

- **Student Loans for College**

- **Education Tax Incentives**

- **Tax Capacity**

- **Grandparents and Relatives Resources**

- **Controlling the Cost of College**

- **Cash Flow for College and Retirement**

- **Parent Loans for College**

- **College and Retirement Investments**

- **13 Step to Solving the College and Retirement Dilemma**

120 W. Main St., Suite 405, Van Wert, Ohio 45891   Ph. (800) 306-6340

www.CSILLC.org